OVAL OFFICE
Occult

OVAL OFFICE
Occult

True Stories of
White House Weirdness

Brian M. Thomsen

**Andrews McMeel
Publishing, LLC**
Kansas City

08 09 10 11 12 MLT 10 9 8 7 6 5 4 3 2

ISBN-13: 978-0-7407-7386-0
ISBN-10: 0-7407-7386-0

Library of Congress Control Number: 2008925903

www.andrewsmcmeel.com

To the memories of

Fred Thomsen the II, Fred Thomsen the III, Isabelle Lincoln, Robert Lincoln, Michael Lincoln, Martin Miller, and Terry Malley, who all now have the answers to questions we discussed.

Contents

Contents

Author's Note

In an attempt to maintain a nonpartisan/apolitical presentation in this volume, whenever appropriate I have tried to provide profiles for the presidents as encapsulated by the official biographers at www.whitehouse.gov.

CONGRESS,

DECLARATION

BY THE REPRESENTATIVES OF THE

UNITED STATES OF AMERICA

IN GENERAL CONGRESS ASSEMBLED.

Introduction

It is chimerically appropriate that Halloween and Election Day fall so close together, as politics is sometimes the most irrational, illogical, and basically unbelievable, yet intrinsically necessary, element of ruling and managing the great democratic republic of the United States.

The frequent excuse "It was just politics" immediately sets aside the allegations and opinions prior to an election so the newly elected representatives of the majority of American voters can get around to legislating the affairs of state.

It's simply incredible . . . and that's on a normal basis.

Yet even amid the incredulity of the process there have still been matters that have been just plain weird.

Maybe it has something to do with the geographic locale or perhaps the interests of the locals?

In August 1944 a certain newspaper ran a news story titled PRIEST FREES MT. RAINIER BOY REPORTED HELD IN DEVIL'S GRIP.

That story caught the attention of a junior at Georgetown University who eventually used the facts of that case as the basis for a best-selling novel.

The student was William Peter Blatty, the novel was *The Exorcist*, and the newspaper that carried that occult story as news was none

other than the *Washington Post* . . . thus further supporting the homo-
geneity of the occult and the city, or in slightly more poetic terms "the
devil and the District."

Indeed, Washington, D.C., was chosen as our seat of government
because at the time it was considered a rather hellish place of ungodly
humidity and monstrous flies and mosquitoes. The idea behind this pur-
gatorial choice was to make it so that those who were involved in govern-
ing would come to town and get the people's business done as quickly as
possible so as to facilitate their exodus to more favorable locales without
due delay. Moreover, those who were *not* directly involved in such matters (those we might now label "outside interest groups") might think
twice about visiting the seat to seize an opportunity to wield influence.

Probably the founding fathers never considered that the city would
become a tourist destination, or that the amenities of indoor plumbing
and central air conditioning would lead to the capital becoming livable
year-round.

For the modern visitor the city breathes history.

The so-called Spirit of '76 is indeed alive and well, and when it comes
to other spirits, there is a good chance that it is by no means alone.

A city that acts as the seat of government takes on the character of that
government, and of course that government takes on the character of
the people charged with running it on a day-to-day basis, the good and
the bad, the present and the past.

They may be doing the people's business, but make no bones about
it, Washington is *their* workplace, just as the White House is not just
the president's place of business, but his place of residence as well.
Presidents are people too—men of the left and of the right, of integrity and of adultery, knowledge smart and cunning smart . . . and, of
course, covering the widest possible spectrum of beliefs.

Indeed, some American presidents haven't just made the headlines in the *New York Times* and *Wall Street Journal* but in the *Weekly World News* and the *Fortean Times* as well.

Consider the following questions:

- Do presidents believe in UFOs?
- Has the White House ever officially sanctioned a séance?
- Have certain presidents expressed an unwillingness to leave the executive residence after both their terms of office and their lives have expired?
- Why do age-old conspiracies and secret societies of the founding fathers still provide fodder for modern-day best-sellers?

Our chief executives have not been strangers to matters of the occult—from the first presidential founding father, George Washington, right up to today.

Some of these occult matters have been based on rumors and suppositions.

Some have been based on hearsay.

Some have even been made up out of whole cloth and later exposed as the hoaxes they were.

Still others exist in the gray area between observers' accounts and cold, hard facts.

Some have even provided creative fodder for recent best-sellers and historical mythmaking.

Ghosts, conspiracies, secret societies, even a vampire, have all been linked to the inhabitants of the White House.

Now, it is not the purpose of this volume to endorse any specific beliefs or provide a stamp of approval/veracity on any of the matters covered. The question of what actually happened is perhaps better left to the witnesses and those with answers far beyond the ken of mortal men. What this volume has attempted to do is provide the reader with as much contemporaneous corroboration as possible to the events and subjects at hand.

Sometimes they are excerpts from memoirs, other times news stories, and still other times oral accounts that may have been put on the record as matters of hearsay.

Remember the definition of the word *occult,* at least according to *Webster's,* is "hidden or secret," and one thing you can say about Washington, D.C., and our government is that they are indeed filled with secrets, in the Oval Office and perhaps even farther beyond.

Occult

DEFINITION

supernatural or magic: relating to or characteristic of magic, witchcraft, or supernatural phenomena

not understandable: not capable of being understood by ordinary human beings

secret: secret or known only to the initiated

hidden

difficult to see

QUESTION:
Are the supposed ghosts at the
White House usually friendly?

GARY WALTERS
(Chief Usher for the White House):

Absolutely. The presidents that I have worked
for have all indicated a feeling of the previous
occupants of the White House and have all
talked about drawing strength from the fact that
the previous presidents have lived here. That is a
positive ghost story!

From *Ask the White House* online Q&A session on
October 31, 2003

Oval Office

Occult

GEORGE WASHINGTON

The Visions of Washington

According to David L. Holmes in his volume *The Faiths of the Founding Fathers:*

"Washington was baptized and raised in the Established Church of Virginia. . . . By the standards of the eighteenth century, Washington was religiously active. As an officer prior to the Revolution, he read services for his soldiers when no chaplain was available and required officers and men not on duty to attend. He scrupulously observed the fast days of the Church of England. . . . He served as a vestryman and churchwarden. . . . From the reports of visitors at Mount Vernon, he occasionally said grace at the table. . . . Washington sometimes worshipped in churches of other denominations, but he normally attended Anglican and Episcopalian churches."

Thus to all apparent evidence, the first president of the United States was fairly conventional in his beliefs, nonheretical, and at least moderately devout, as one would expect of a man who rose through the ranks of the military, managed a moderate plantation, and ascended to the executive ranks of government without any tarrying in so-called politics.

Yet, for some reason, this religiously conventional fellow has been linked to numerous matters of the occult ranging from Indian prophecies to Masonic conspiracies to postdeath spectral appearances.

True, as with the fictional mythmaking of so-called biographer Parson Weems (who invented the Washington cherry-tree/never-tell-a-lie legend), much of the paranormal legacy may indeed be tall tales. And in the quote often attributed to director John Ford but more correctly attributed to the screenwriters of *The Man Who Shot Liberty Valance* (James Warner Bellah, Willis Goldbeck, and Dorothy M. Johnson, who wrote the underlying story), "when the legend becomes fact, print the legend."

The Indian Prophecy

Washington's first paranormal incident actually predates the American Revolution, back to his days as a young British officer under General Edward Braddock during the French and Indian war. The story of the so-called Indian Prophecy is as follows:

IT WAS IN 1770, that Colonel Washington, accompanied by Doctor James Craik, and a considerable party of hunters, woodsmen, and others, proceeded to the Kanawha with a view to explore the country, and make surveys of extensive and valuable bodies of lands. At that time of day, the Kanawha was several hundred miles remote from the frontier settlements, and only accessible by Indian paths, which wound through the passes of the mountains.

In those wild and unfrequented regions, the party formed a camp on the bank of the river, consisting of rudely-constructed wigwams or shelters, from which they issued to explore and survey those alluvial tracts, now forming the most fertile and best inhabited parts of the west of Virginia.

This romantic camp, though far removed from the homes of civilization, possessed very many advantages. The great abundance of various kinds of game, in its vicinity, afforded a sumptuous larder, while a few luxuries of foreign growth, which had been brought on the baggage horses, made the adventurers as comfortable as they could reasonably desire.

One day when resting in camp from the fatigues attendant on so arduous an enterprise, a party of Indians led by a trader, were discovered. No recourse was had to arms, for peace in great measure reigned on the frontier; the border warfare which so long had harassed the unhappy settlers, had principally subsided, and the savage driven farther and farther back, as the settlements advanced, had sufficiently felt the power of the whites, to view them with fear, as well as hate. Again, the approach of this party was anything but hostile, and the appearance of the trader, a being half savage, half civilized, made it certain that the mission was rather of peace than war.

They halted at a short distance, and the interpreter advancing, declared that he was conducting a party, which consisted of a grand sachem, and some attendant warriors; that the chief was a very great man among the northwestern tribes, and the same who commanded the Indians on the fall of Braddock, sixteen years before, that hearing of the visit of Colonel Washington to the western country, this chief had set out on a mission, the object of which himself would make known.

The colonel received the ambassador with courtesy, and having put matters in camp in the best possible order for the reception of such distinguished visitors, which so short a notice would allow, the strangers were introduced.

Among the colonists were some fine, tall, and manly figures, but so soon as the sachem approached, he in a moment pointed out the hero of the Monongahela, from among the group, although sixteen years had elapsed since he had seen him, and then only in the tumult and fury of battle. The Indian was of a lofty stature, and of a dignified and imposing appearance.

The usual salutations were going round, when it was observed, that the grand chief, although perfectly familiar with every other person present, preserved toward Colonel Washington the most reverential deference. It was in vain that the colonel extended his hand, the Indian drew back, with the most impressive marks of awe and respect. A last effort was made to induce a discourse, by resorting to the delight of the savages—ardent spirit—which the colonel having tasted, offered to his guest; the Indian bowed his head in submission, but wetted not his lips. Tobacco, for the use of which Washington always had the utmost abhorrence, was next tried, the colonel taking a single puff to the great annoyance of his feelings, and then offering the calumet to the chief, who touched not the symbol of savage friendship. The banquet being now ready, the colonel did the honors of the feast, and placing the great man at his side, helped him plentifully, but the Indian fed not at the board. Amazement now possessed the company, and an intense anxiety became apparent, as to the issue of so extraordinary an adventure. The council fire was kindled, when the grand sachem addressed our Washington to the following effect: "I am a chief, and the ruler over many tribes. My influence extends to the waters of the great lakes, and to the far blue mountains. I have traveled a long and weary path, that I might see the young warrior of the great battle. It was on the day, when the white man's blood, mixed with the streams of our forest, that I first beheld this chief: I called to my young men and said, mark yon tall and daring warrior? He is not of the red-coat tribe—he hath an Indian's wisdom, and his warriors fight as we do—himself is alone exposed. Quick, let your aim be certain, and he dies. Our rifles were leveled, rifles which, but for him, knew not how to miss—'twas all in vain, a power mightier far than we, shielded him from harm. He can not die in battle. I am old, and soon shall be gathered to the great council-fire of my fathers, in the land of shades, but ere I go, there is a something, bids me speak, in the voice of prophecy. Listen! The

Great Spirit protects that man, and guides his destinies—he must become the chief of nations, and a people yet unborn, will hail him as the founder of a mighty empire." The savage ceased, his oracle delivered, his prophetic mission fulfilled, he retired to muse in silence, upon that wonder-working Spirit, which is dark.

Untutored mind saw oft in clouds, and heard Him in the wind. Night coming on, the children of the forest spread their blankets, and were soon buried in sleep. At early dawn they bid adieu to the camp, and were seen slowly winding their way toward the distant haunts of their tribe.

The effects which this mysterious and romantic adventure had upon the provincials, were as various as the variety of character which composed the party. All eyes were turned on him, to whom the oracle had been addressed, but from his ever-serene and thoughtful countenance, nothing could be discovered: still all this was strange, "'twas passive strange." On the mind of Doctor James Craik, a most deep and lasting impression was made, and in the war of the Revolution it became a favorite theme with him, particularly after any perilous action, in which his friend and commander had been peculiarly exposed, as the battles of Princeton, Germantown, and Monmouth. On the latter occasion, as we have elsewhere observed, Doctor Craik expressed his great faith in the Indian's prophecy.

"Gentlemen," he said, to some of the officers, "recollect what I have often told you, of the old Indian's prophecy. Yes, I do believe, a Great Spirit protects that man—and that one day or other, honored and beloved, he will be the chief of our nation, as he is now our general, our father, and our friend. Never mind the enemy, they can not kill him, and while he lives, our cause will never die."

During the engagement on the following day, while Washington was speaking to a favorite officer, I think the brave and valued Colonel Hartley, of the Pennsylvania line, a cannon ball struck just at his horse's feet, throwing the dirt in his face, and over his clothes, the general continued giving his orders, without noticing the derangement of his toilette. The officers present, several of whom were of the party the preceding evening, looked at each other with anxiety. The chief of the medical staff, pleased with the proof of his prediction, and in reminiscence of what had passed the night before, pointed toward heaven, which was noticed by the others, with a gratifying smile of acknowledgment.

Of the brave and valued Colonel Hartley, it is said, that the commander-in-chief sent for him in the heat of an engagement, and addressed him as follows: "I have sent for you, colonel, to employ you on a serious piece of service. The state of our affairs, renders it necessary, that a part of this army should be sacrificed, for the welfare of the whole. You command an efficient corps (a fine regiment of Germans from York and Lancaster counties). I know you well, and have, therefore, selected you to perform this important and serious duty. You will take such a position, and defend it to the last extremity."

The colonel received this appointment to a forlorn hope, with a smile of exultation, and bowing, replied: "Your Excellency does me too much honor; your orders shall be obeyed to the letter," and repaired to his post.

I will not be positive as to the location of this anecdote, having heard it from the old people of the Revolution many years ago, but think it occurred on the field of Monmouth—but of this I am not certain. I have a hundred times seen Colonel Hartley received in the halls of the great president, where so many Revolutionary worthies were made welcome, and to none was the hand of honored and friendly recollection more feelingly offered; on none did the merit-discerning eye of the chief appear to beam with more pleasure, than on Hartley of York.

Now, what separates this incident of prophecy from the Washington mythologizing of such "true-life" tale-spinners as Parson Weems, is the authorship, namely the first president's adopted son George Washington Parke Custis in collaboration with the former physician general of the U.S. Army (and close personal friend and personal physician of the president) Dr. Craik, who indeed served with Washington during the Battle of the Great Meadow and the surrender of Fort Neccessity, and much later tended to the failing former president during his last hours on his deathbed . . . and is, incidentally, the same Dr. Craik who is mentioned in the passage.

Whether the event happened is obviously subject to debate, and the fact that Custis later turned this incident into a dramatic touring play for profit (titled *The Indian Prophecy; or Visions of Glory,* no less) probably has to be taken into account, and usually is by those skeptical of the paranormal and prophecy.

The Vision at Valley Forge

The second visionary incident of the first president allegedly took place during the American Revolution, and like the so-called Indian Prophecy casts the then general as the guiding light for a new republic that would be entering troubled times. This time, however, rather than the "heathen" words of a savage invoking some Great Spirit, the messenger is decidedly angelic, and her message equally decidedly Christian.

The time was the winter of 1778, and the place was his military headquarters at Valley Forge during some of the darkest days of the revolution. According to the tale as allegedly related by Washington himself:

THIS AFTERNOON, AS I was sitting at this table engaged in preparing a dispatch, something seemed to disturb me. Looking up, I beheld standing opposite me a singularly beautiful female. So astonished was I, for I had given strict orders not to be disturbed, that it was some moments before I found language to inquire the cause of her presence. A second, a third and even a fourth time did I repeat my question, but received no answer from my mysterious visitor except a slight raising of her eyes.

By this time I felt strange sensations spreading through me. I would have risen but the riveted gaze of the being before me rendered volition impossible. I assayed once more to address her, but my tongue had become useless, as though it had become paralyzed.

A new influence, mysterious, potent, irresistible, took possession of me. All I could do was to gaze steadily, vacantly at my unknown visitor. Gradually the surrounding atmosphere seemed as if it had become filled with sensations, and luminous. Everything about me seemed to rarify, the mysterious visitor herself becoming more airy and yet more distinct to my sight than before. I now began to feel as one dying, or rather to experience the sensations which I have sometimes imagined accompany dissolution. I did not think, I did not reason, I did not move; all were alike impossible. I was only conscious of gazing fixedly, vacantly at my companion.

Presently I heard a voice saying, "Son of the Republic, look and learn," while at the same time my visitor extended her arm eastwardly. I now beheld a heavy white vapor at some distance rising fold upon fold. This gradually dissipated, and I looked upon a strange scene. Before me lay spread out in one vast plain all the countries of the world; Europe, Asia, Africa and America. I saw rolling and tossing between Europe and America the billows of the Atlantic, and between Asia and America lay the Pacific.

"Son of the Republic," said the same mysterious voice as before, "look and learn." At that moment I beheld a dark, shadowy being, like an angel, standing, or rather floating in mid-air, between Europe and America. Dipping water out of the ocean in the hollow of each hand, he sprinkled some upon America with his right hand, while with his left hand he cast some on Europe. Immediately a cloud raised from these countries, and joined in mid-ocean. For a while it remained stationary, and then moved slowly westward, until it enveloped America in its murky folds. Sharp flashes of lightning gleamed through it at intervals, and I heard the smothered groans and cries of the American people.

A second time the angel dipped water from the ocean, and sprinkled it out as before. The dark cloud was then drawn back to the ocean, in whose heaving billows it sank from view. A third time I heard the mysterious voice saying, "Son of the Republic, look and learn." I cast my eyes upon America and beheld villages and towns and cities springing up one after another until the whole land from the Atlantic to the Pacific was dotted with them.

Again, I heard the mysterious voice say, "Son of the Republic, the end of the century cometh, look and learn." At this the dark shadowy angel turned his face southward, and from Africa I saw an ill-omened specter approach our land. It flitted slowly over every town and city of the latter. The inhabitants presently set themselves in battle array against each other. As I continued looking I saw a bright angel, on whose brow rested a crown of light, on which was traced the word "Union," bearing the American flag which he placed between the divided nation, and said, "Remember ye are brethren." Instantly, the inhabitants, casting from them their weapons became friends once more, and united around the National Standard.

And again I heard the mysterious voice saying, "Son of the Republic, look and learn." At this the dark, shadowy angel placed a trumpet to his mouth, and blew three distinct blasts; and taking water from the ocean, he sprinkled it upon Europe, Asia and Africa. Then my eyes beheld a fearful scene: from each of these countries arose thick, black clouds that were soon joined into one. Throughout this mass there gleamed a dark red light by which I saw hordes of armed men, who, moving with the cloud, marched by land and sailed by sea to America. Our country was enveloped in this volume of cloud, and I saw these vast armies devastate the whole country and burn the villages, towns and cities that I beheld springing up. As my ears listened to the thundering of the cannon, clashing of swords, and the shouts and cries of millions in mortal combat, I heard again the mysterious voice saying, "Son of the Republic, look and learn." When the voice had ceased, the dark shadowy angel placed his trumpet once more to his mouth, and blew a long and fearful blast.

Instantly a light as of a thousand suns shone down from above me, and pierced and broke into fragments the dark cloud which enveloped America. At the same moment the angel upon whose head still shone the word Union, and who bore our national flag in one hand and a sword in the other, descended from the heavens attended by legions of white spirits. These immediately joined the inhabitants of America, who I perceived were well nigh overcome, but who immediately taking courage again, closed up their broken ranks and renewed the battle.

Again, amid the fearful noise of the conflict, I heard the mysterious voice saying, "Son of the Republic, look and learn." As the voice ceased, the shadowy angel for the last time dipped water from the ocean and sprinkled it upon America. Instantly the dark cloud rolled back, together with the armies it had brought, leaving the inhabitants of the land victorious!

Then once more I beheld the villages, towns and cities springing up where I had seen them before, while the bright angel, planting the azure standard he had brought in the midst of them, cried with a loud voice, "While the stars remain, and the heavens send down dew upon the earth, so long shall the Union last." And taking from his brow the crown on which blazoned the word "UNION," he placed it upon the Standard while the people, kneeling down, said, "Amen."

The scene instantly began to fade and dissolve, and I at last saw nothing but the rising, curling vapor I at first beheld. This also disappearing, I found myself once more gazing upon the mysterious visitor, who, in the same voice I had heard before, said, "Son of the Republic, what you have seen is thus interpreted: three great perils will come upon the Republic. The most fearful is the third, but in this greatest conflict the whole world united shall not prevail against her. Let every child of the Republic learn to live for his God, his land and the Union." With these words the vision vanished, and I started from my seat and felt that I had seen a vision wherein had been shown to me the birth, progress and destiny of the United States.

For most skeptics the question of Washington's authorship of this reminiscence of a paranormal visitation and prophetic/clairvoyant vision of the nation's upcoming history has been pretty much discredited. It appeared in the *National Tribune* in vol. 4, no. 12, December 1880, as an account of the "Vision of Washington" at Valley Forge as supposedly told by a gentleman named Anthony Sherman, who was at Valley Forge during the winter of 1777–78.

Sherman supposedly introduced this account as follows:

"You doubtless heard the story of Washington's going to the thicket to pray in secret for aid and comfort from God, the interposition of whose Divine Providence brought us safely through the darkest days of tribulation. One day, I remember it well, when the chilly winds whistled through the leafless trees, though the sky was cloudless and the sun shone brightly, he remained in his quarters nearly all the afternoon alone. When he came out, I noticed that his face was a shade paler than usual. There seemed to be something on his mind of more than ordinary importance. Returning just after dusk, he dispatched an orderly to the quarters who was presently in attendance. After a preliminary conversation of about an hour, Washington, gazing upon his companion with that strange look of dignity which he alone commanded, related the event that occurred that day."

All well and good as related by an eyewitness, but unfortunately there is no record that Anthony Sherman actually served at Valley Forge, let alone witnessed or recorded the actual event. Moreover, the actual author credited by the *National Tribune* is Wesley Bradshaw, who supposedly stumbled on Anthony Sherman's account, accepting its veracity without any skepticism whatsoever.

What is troubling to historians is that Bradshaw's account of Sherman's account is the first appearance of this incident in the Washington legacy canon. It is entirely possible that Bradshaw never questioned its credibility because he was in fact its sole author, having incorporated the mystical prophecy motif of the Custis and Craik account with the more conventional Christian account of the general praying in the snow at Valley Forge as related in "The Diary and Remembrances" of the Reverend Nathaniel Randolph Snowden (1770–1851), which is related as follows:

I KNEW PERSONALLY THE celebrated Quaker Potts who saw Gen'l Washington alone in the woods at prayer. I got it from himself, myself. Weems mentioned it in his history of Washington, but I got it from the man myself, as follows: I was riding with him (Mr. Potts) in Montgomery County, Penn'a near to the Valley Forge, where the army lay during the war of ye Revolution. Mr. Potts was a Senator in our State & a Whig. I told him I was agreeably surprised to find him a friend to his country as the Quakers were mostly Tories. He said, "It was so and I was a rank Tory once, for I never believed that America c'd proceed against Great Britain whose fleets and armies covered the land and ocean, but something very extraordinary converted me to the Good Faith!" "What was that," I inquired? "Do you see that woods, & that plain." It was about a quarter of a mile off from the place

we were riding, as it happened. "There," said he, "laid the army of
Washington. It was a most distressing time of ye war, and all were
for giving up the Ship but that great and good man. In that woods
pointing to a close in view, I heard a plaintive sound as, of a man at
prayer. I tied my horse to a sapling & went quietly into the woods
& to my astonishment I saw the great George Washington on his
knees alone, with his sword on one side and his cocked hat on the
other. He was at Prayer to the God of the Armies, beseeching to
interpose with his Divine aid, as it was ye Crisis, & the cause of the
country, of humanity & of the world.

"Such a prayer I never heard from the lips of man. I left him
alone praying.

"I went home & told my wife. I saw a sight and heard today
what I never saw or heard before, and just related to her what I had
seen & heard & observed. We never thought a man c'd be a soldier
& a Christian, but if there is one in the world, it is Washington. She
also was astonished. We thought it was the cause of God, & America
could prevail." He then to me put out his right hand & said "I turned
right about and became a Whig."

I felt much impressed in his presence and reflected upon the
hand and wonderful Providence of God in raising him up and quali-
fying him with so many rare qualities and virtues for the good of
this country and the world. Washington was not only brave and
talented, but a truly excellent and pious man of God and of prayer.
He always retired before a battle and in any emergency for prayer
and direction.

When the army lay at Morristown, the Rev. Dr. Jones, adminis-
tered the sacrament of ye Lord's supper. Washington came forward
at ye head of all his officers and took his seat at ye 1st table, & took
of ye bread and wine, the Symbols of Christ's broken body and shed
blood, to do this in remembrance of ye L J C & thus professed himself a Christian & a disciple of the blessed Jesus.

This scene has further been immortalized in numerous portraits and been cited by numerous people of faith as proof positive of Washington's devoutness, yet the invocation of the discredited Washington authority Parson Weems tends to make the provenance of this account just as dubious as the more paranormal and less Christian accounts that have preceded it. One does not have to question the veracity of the good Reverend Nathaniel Randolph Snowden, but merely be skeptical of the hearsay account credited by him to the Quaker Isaac Potts, a source no less verifiably substantiated than Wesley Bradshaw's Mr. Sherman.

To further put it all into perspective is the stance taken by the Parks Department, responsible for maintaining the historic site: "One of the legends or myths of Valley Forge is that Washington prayed for his country here. We do not say that he did not pray at Valley Forge, there simply is an open question as to how he did so and if he actually was witnessed in prayer."

. . . which basically places this iconic moment of "American history" in the same category as its more occult brethren.

Visions of Washington during the Civil War

Washington's paranormal role in American history didn't stop with his death. One major Union general during the Civil War apparently was visited by the specter of the first president, as evidenced by the following article in the *Evening Courier,* Portland, Maine, March 8, 1862:

WHEN 1862 DAWNED, few realized how dire the situation was for the Republic. . . . General George Brinton McClellan went to Washington, D.C., to take over command of the United States Army. At 2 A.M. on the third night after his arrival, he was working over his maps and studying the reports of the scouts when a feeling of intense weariness caused him to lean his head on his folded arms on the table where he fell asleep.

About ten minutes later the locked door was suddenly thrown open, someone strode right up to him and in a voice of power and authority said: "General McClellan, do you sleep at your post? Rouse you, or ere it can be prevented, the foe will be in Washington."

In his published article General McClellan described his strange feelings. . . . He seemed suspended in infinite space and the voice came from a hollow distance all about him. . . . The furnishings and walls of the room had vanished leaving only the table covered with maps before him. But he found himself gazing upon a living map of America including the entire area from the Mississippi River to the Atlantic Ocean.

McClellan was aware of the being that stood beside him, but could only identify it as a vapor having the vague outline of a man. As he looked at the living map the general was at first amazed and then elated as he saw the troop movements and a complete pattern of the enemy's lines and distribution of forces. This knowledge would enable him to terminate the war speedily. But this elation dissolved as he saw the enemy occupy positions he had intended occupying within the next few days. He realized his plans were known to the enemy.

At this realization the voice spoke again: "General McClellan, you have been betrayed! And had not God willed otherwise, ere the sun of tomorrow had set, the Confederate flag would have waved above the capitol and your own grave. But note what you see. Your time is short."

McClellan did note what he saw on the living map, transferring it to the paper map on his table. When this was done he became aware that the figure near him had increased in light and glory until it shone as the noonday sun. He raised his eyes and looked into the face of George Washington.

With sublime and gentle dignity Washington said, "General Mc-Clellan, while yet in the flesh I beheld the birth of the American Republic. It was indeed a hard and bloody one, but God's blessing was upon the nation, and therefore, through this, her first great struggle for existence, He sustained her and with His mighty hand brought her out triumphantly. A century has not passed since then, and yet the child Republic has taken her position of peer with nations whose pages of history extend for ages into the past. She has, since those dark days, by the favor of God, greatly prospered. And now, by very reason of this prosperity, she has been brought to her second great struggle. This is by far the most perilous ordeal she has to endure; passing as she is from childhood to opening maturity, she is called on to accomplish that vast result, self-conquest; to learn that important lesson, self-control, self rule, that in the future will place her in the van of power and civilization. . . .

"But her mission will not then be finished; for ere another century shall have gone by, the oppressors of the whole earth, hating and envying her exaltation, shall join themselves together and raise up their hands against her. But if she still be found worthy of her high calling they shall surely be discomfited, and then will be ended her third and last great struggle for existence. Thenceforth shall the Republic go on, increasing in power and goodness, until her borders shall end only in the remotest corners of the earth, and the whole earth shall beneath her shadowing wing become a Universal Republic. Let her in her prosperity, however, remember the Lord her God, let her trust be always in Him, and she shall never be confounded."

Washington raised his hand over McClellan's head in blessing, a peal of thunder rumbled through space; the general awoke with a start. He was in his room with his maps spread out on the table before him, but as he looked at them [to his astonishment, he saw] the maps were covered with marks and figures he had made during the vision . . . this convinced him that his dream or vision was real and was from above.

He set about immediately . . . to thwart the enemy's plan, riding his horse from camp to camp to implement the changes at once. The Confederate Army was so near that President Lincoln could hear the rumble of their artillery sitting in the study at the White House.

McClellan's action saved the capitol early in 1862, and saved the Republic from the second peril. The first "peril" had been the Revolutionary War.

Thus the Union was saved and General McClellan concludes his account of his Vision with these words:

"Our beloved, glorious Washington shall again rest quietly, sweetly in his tomb, until perhaps the end of the Prophetic Century approaches that is to bring the Republic to a third and final struggle, when he may once more laying aside the crements of Mount Vernon, become a Messenger of Succor and Peace from the Great Ruler, who has all Nations of this Earth in His keeping.

"But the future is too vast for our comprehension; we are children of the present. When peace shall have folded her bright wings and settled our land, the strange, unearthly map marked while the Spirit eyes of Washington looked down, shall be preserved among American Archives as a precious reminder to the American nation what in their second great struggle for existence, they owe to God and the Glorified Spirit of Washington. Verily the works of God are above the understanding of man!"

Now, George McClellan was by no means a shrinking violet when it came to the press, particularly when he tried to trumpet his own stint as general-in-chief of the Union Army in an effort to replace then commander in chief President Abraham Lincoln through the 1864 presidential election where he ran as the Democratic candidate.

The veracity of the visitation might be called into question except that there is no evidence that McClellan ever refuted it in the press or otherwise at its time of original publication or at any of the subsequent times it was reprinted.

It is wholly unlikely that it escaped his notice, as it was alluded to in numerous anti-Lincoln articles (including one related to spiritualism that is referenced in chapter 9, "The Presidents and Their Spiritual Advisers") and indeed might have been a cleverly masked political attempt at inferring that there was a postdeath endorsement of his candidacy by the revered and deceased first president.

Over the course of his life, despite his failure to unseat Lincoln, McClellan remained in the public eye until his death in 1885, attaining numerous political positions and authoring several works, including a self-justifying/-aggrandizing autobiography that was published posthumously . . . yet, despite the numerous opportunities, he failed to refute the tale, including when it was recirculated in 1880 during his term as governor of New Jersey.

The papers then related the story as follows:

GENERAL MCCLELLAN'S VISION OF
GEORGE WASHINGTON

According to the *National Tribune,* December 1880

IN A STRATEGIC MOMENT in the Civil War, General George B. McClellan, who had been called by President Lincoln to take charge of the shattered Union forces, fell asleep at his desk.

He had scarcely been asleep a moment, when it seemed that he was awake, and the whole room was filled with a radiant light. Suddenly, out of the light, he heard a voice, and later saw the face of George Washington, who gave him warning that the Confederate troops were on their way to take the Capitol.

Because of this, with something akin to supernatural knowledge, General McClellan was able to pursue Gen. Robert E. Lee, and stop the northern invasion by the Confederacy at Antietam, September, 1862. This vision was first reported in the Portland *Evening Courier* at the time the tide turned for the Union forces. Since that time, it has been written as a warning to the American people again and again because of its reference to the last war which will be fought toward the end of this century . . . when a great conflict could arise with the "oppressors of the whole earth" in which our land could be involved.

In General McClellan's account of this vision, he relates that the voice of Washington, with penetrating clarity, called out to him:

"General McClellan, do you sleep at your post? Rouse you, or 'ere it can be prevented, the foe will be in Washington! . . . You have been betrayed, and had God not willed it otherwise, 'ere the sun of tomorrow had set, the Confederate flag would have waved above the Capitol and your own grave. But note what you see. Your time is short!"

In this strange dream state, General McClellan seemed to see a living map of all the troop positions—and with a pencil at hand, he began to copy down all that he saw—the positions of the Confederate troops as they marched toward Washington; the maneuvers which they planned in the future. After the warning of the immediate peril which faced the Union, the splendor of Washington became even greater as he spoke of the days ahead in this, the 20th century, when other perils could befall our nation.

"General McClellan, while yet in the flesh, I beheld the birth of the America Republic. It was indeed a hard and bloody one, but God's blessing was upon the nation, and, therefore, through this, her first great struggle for existence.

"He sustained her, and with His mighty hand, He brought her out triumphantly.

"A century has not passed since then, and yet the child Republic has taken her position of peer with nations whose pages of history extend for ages into the past. She has, since those dark days, by the favor of God, greatly prospered. And now, by the very reason of that prosperity, has she been brought to her second great struggle.

"This is by far the most perilous ordeal she has to endure, passing as she is from childhood to open maturity, she is called on to accomplish that vast result, Self-Conquest; to learn that important lesson—self-control, self-rule, that in the future will place her in the van of power and civilization." It is here that all the nations have hitherto failed, and she, too—the Republic of the earth, had not God willed other wise—would by tomorrow's sunset have been a heap of stones, cast up over the final grave of human liberty. But! her cries have come up out of the borders like sweet incense into heaven. She shall be saved! Then, shall peace be upon her, and prosperity shall fill her with joy.

"But her mission will not be finished, for 'ere another century shall have gone by, THE OPPRESSORS OF THE WHOLE EARTH, hating and envying her exaltation, shall join themselves together and raise up their hands against her.

"But if she be found worthy of her calling, they shall be truly discomfited, and then will be ended her third and last struggle for existence. Henceforth, shall the Republic go on, increasing in goodness and power until her borders shall end only in the remotest corners of the earth, and the whole earth shall, beneath her shadowy wings, become A UNIVERSAL REPUBLIC!"

Upon hearing these words, General McClellan awoke to find the markings and symbols of the Confederate maneuvers upon his own maps as if his dream-pencil had actually placed them there. In his account of this strange precognitive experience, General McClellan wrote:

". . . Our beloved, glorious Washington shall rest . . . until perhaps the end of the Prophetic Century approaches, that is to bring the Republic to a third and final struggle when he may once more . . . become a Messenger of Succor and Peace from the Great Ruler, who has all nations in his keeping . . ."

A few changes over time, but consistent with the earlier account.

And if this wasn't enough there is yet another Civil War appearance by the first president, or at least a rumor of one, according to a different officer present at the Battle of Gettysburg. In his article "Through Blood and Fire at Gettysburg" (published in *Hearst's Magazine* June 1913), Joshua Chamberlain relates the following prebattle scene:

NIGHTFALL BROUGHT US TO Hanover, Pennsylvania, and to a halt. And it was the evening of the first day of July, 1863. All day we had been marching north from Maryland, searching and pushing out on all roads for the hoped-for collision with Lee eagerly, hurriedly, yet cautiously, with skirmishers and flankers out to sound the first challenge, and our main body ready for the call. Fanwise our divisions had been spread out to cover Washington, but more was at stake than the capital city of the Union: there was that important political and international question, the recognition of the Southern Confederacy as independent by France and England. This recognition, denying the very contentions of the North from the beginning would have been almost fatal to it. And Lee need not win a decided victory in the field to bring about the recognition: his capture and occupation of an important and strategic point in the North would have been enough.

All day, ever and again, we had seen detachments of Lee's cavalry; even as we passed an outlying field to our encampment the red slanting sunlight fell softly across the grim relics of a cavalry fight of the afternoon; the survivors of which had swept on, and pursuing.

Worn and famished we stacked arms in camping order, hoping to bivouac beside them, and scampered like madcaps for those two prime factors of a desultory supper—water and fence-rails; for the finding of which the Yankee volunteer has an aptitude which should be ranked among the spiritual intuitions, though in their old-school theology most farmers of our acquaintance were inclined to reckon the aptitude among the carnal appetites of the totally depraved. Some of the forage wagons had now got up, and there was a brief rally at their tail ends for quick justice to be dispensed. But the unregenerate fires had hardly blackened the coffee-dippers, and the hardtack hardly been hammered into working order by the bayonet shanks, when everything was stopped short by whispers of disaster away on the left: the enemy had struck our columns at Gettysburg, and driven it back with terrible loss; Reynolds, the commander, had been killed, and the remnant scarcely able to hold on to the hillsides unless rescue came before morning. These were only rumors flitting owl-like, in the gathering shadows. We could not quite believe them, but they deepened our mood.

Suddenly the startling bugle-call from unseen headquarters! "The General!" it rang! "To the march! No moment of delay!"

Word was coming, too. Staff officers dashed from corps, to division, to brigade, to regiment, to battery and the order flew like the hawk, and not the owl. "To Gettysburg!" it said, a forced march of sixteen miles. But what forced it? And what opposed? Not supper, nor sleep, nor sore feet and aching limbs.

In a moment, the whole corps was in marching order; rest, rations, earth itself forgotten; one thought,—to be first on that Gettysburg road. The iron-faced veterans were transformed to boys. They insisted on starting out with colors flying, so that even the night might know what manner of men were coming to redeem the day.

All things, even the most common, were magnified and made mysterious by the strange spell of night. At a turn of the road a staff-officer, with an air of authority, told each colonel as he came up, that McClellan was in command again, and riding ahead of us on the road. Then wild cheers rolled from the crowding column into the brooding sky, and the earth shook under the quickened tread. *Now from a dark angle of the roadside came a whisper, whether from earthly or unearthly voice one cannot feel quite sure, that the august form of Washington had been seen that afternoon at sunset riding over the Gettysburg hills. Let no one smile at me! I half believed it myself,—so did the powers of the other world draw nigh!*

But there were wayside greetings such as we had never met before. We were in a free state, and among friendly people. All along the road, citizens came out to contemplate this martial array with a certain awe, and greet us with hearty welcome. But, most of all, our dark way was illumined by groups of girls in sweet attire gathered on the embowered lawns of modest homes, with lights and banners and flowers, and stirring songs whose import and effect were quite other than impersonal. Those who were not sisters of the muse of song waved their welcome in the ripple of white handkerchiefs—which token the gallant young gentlemen of the staff were prompt to take as summons to parley, and boldly rode up to meet with soft, half-tone scenes under the summer night: those meetings looked much like proposals for exchange of prisoners, or unconditional surrender. And others still, not daring quite so much, but unable to repress the gracious impulse of giving, offered their silent benediction in a cup of water. And we remembered then with what sanction it was that water had been turned to wine in Cana of Galilee!

Chamberlain doesn't actually claim to have interacted with America's first commander in chief, nor does he claim to have actually witnessed the scene himself. Nonetheless, he thought it noteworthy enough to chronicle, and the mention of the nearby presence of McClellan might actually add credence to the other recorded account.

(Author's note: Subsequent to my completing research on this section I discovered mentions of another Washington spectral appearance to a historical person of note. According to legendary ghost hunter Hans Holzer, the first president appeared to John C. Calhoun on the eve of the secession of South Carolina, saying that such an occurrence would be a black mark on the Constitution. Calhoun signed on to the Confederacy anyway and [according to Holzer] "a dark spot appeared on his hand, a spot that would not vanish and for which medical authorities had no adequate explanation." All mentions of this incident trace back to Holzer, and I have not been able to find any contemporary accounts to verify this story beyond the realm of hearsay.)

Harding's Cursed Hope

Warren G. Harding had what was considered by many to be one of the most easily navigated roads to the White House. He was picked as the Republican candidate largely because, in the words of one of his ardent supporters, "he looked like a president"—and it would appear that a vast majority of the electorate agreed. He promised a return to normalcy after the turmoil of the First World War and in 1920 was elected the twenty-ninth president of the United States with an, at the time, overwhelming 60 percent of the popular vote, which was heralded as an unprecedented landslide.

With a people's mandate assured, he was poised to work his will and, in the words of his official White House biography, "eliminated wartime controls and slashed taxes, established a Federal budget system, restored the high protective tariff, and imposed tight limitations upon immigration."

Republicans, their big-business backers, and newspapers hailed Harding as a wise statesman carrying out his campaign promise: "Less government in business and more business in government."

He was poised for greatness . . . so why do most presidential scholars consider him one of our least successful presidents?

Maybe what was good for Harding wasn't good for America, or perhaps the paranormal played a role, specifically a gem whose history predates the formation of the United States and is now associated with a cursed legacy.

The history of the stone which was eventually named the Hope diamond began when the French merchant traveler, Jean Baptiste Tavernier, purchased a 112 3/16-carat diamond. This diamond, which was most likely from the Kollur mine in Golconda, India, was somewhat triangular in shape and crudely cut. Its color was described by Tavernier as a "beautiful violet." . . . The weight of the Hope diamond for many years was reported to be 44.5 carats. In 1974 it was removed from its setting and found actually to weigh 45.52 carats. It is classified as a type IIb diamond, which are semi conductive and usually phosphoresce. The Hope diamond phosphoresces a strong red color, which will last for several seconds after exposure to short wave ultra-violet light. The diamond's blue coloration is attributed to trace amounts of boron in the stone.

Thus begins the Encyclopedia Smithsonian's entry for one of the Smithsonian Institution's most infamous exhibits/holdings.

The gem's legacy dates back to the court of Louis XIV of France, where it was known under such monikers as the "Blue Diamond of the Crown" or the "French Blue." Though it became quite well traveled and passed through many hands, it was only in the early part of the twentieth century that talk of a curse started to circulate.

In an article in the June 25, 1909, issue of the *Times* (London) allegedly written by the newspaper's Paris correspondent, the diamond's cursed infamy is mentioned and a number of supposed owners who came to ignoble ends are listed. According to this legend the diamond was stolen from the eye of an ancient Hindu idol and the idol's worshippers called down a curse on all whose hands the diamond passed through until it was returned to its rightful home.

The legend claimed that the thief died of fever soon after and that his body was torn apart by wolves (historical record shows that he actually lived to age eighty-four, and wolves were not listed as his cause of death).

The Hope Diamond was also blamed for Madame de Montespan's and French finance minister Nicolas Fouquet's falling out of favor with Louis XIV, the beheadings of King Louis XVI and his wife, Marie Antoinette, and the rape, mutilation, and beheading of the Princesse de Lamballe—as well as the unfortunate ends of numerous gem cutters, dealers, thieves, etc., whose existences are all but impossible to confirm.

In 1910 the legendary jeweler Pierre Cartier sold the gem to the American heiress Evalyn Walsh McLean, who became quite enamored with the expensive bauble and proceeded to wear it wherever and whenever she could, including political gatherings, fund-raisers, and meetings she attended with her husband, Edward Beale McLean (the publisher of the *Washington Post*). Evalyn would often allow her friends to try on her favorite piece of jewelry. As luck would have it the Hardings were indeed among the McLeans' circle of friends, and Florence Harding did indeed take advantage of the opportunity to try out her friend's favorite bauble.

The McLean family, it is alleged, did not escape the curse. The firstborn son died in a car crash when he was only nine, the daughter committed suicide at age twenty-five, and after Evalyn's own death, the diamond had to be put up for sale to take care of outstanding family debts.

So what did this have to do with President Harding's downward spiral?

Well, given the social whirl of the White House and the influence of the McLeans in the D.C. circle, it is easy to conclude that the Hardings, once ensconced at 1600 Pennsylvania Avenue, made their first acquaintance with the cursed gem early in Harding's presidential tenure.

And what was the result?

Scandals galore, including the legendary Teapot Dome affair, which involved the accepting of bribes by the secretary of the interior in exchange for the leasing of public oil fields to private interests.

Other scandals included:

- Harding appointee Thomas Miller convicted of accepting bribes
- The head of the Veterans' Bureau embezzling funds while engaging in other illegal activities
- The suicides of at least two aides who were under investigation

Though Harding himself was never directly implicated in any of the scandals, his presidential aura was quickly tarnished and his administration forever stained by its cronyism and corruption.

Harding himself failed to outlive his administration's scandals. Once again quoting from his official White House biography:

"Looking wan and depressed, Harding journeyed westward in the summer of 1923, taking with him his upright Secretary of Commerce, Herbert Hoover. 'If you knew of a great scandal in our administration,' he asked Hoover, 'would you for the good of the country and the party expose it publicly or would you bury it?' Hoover urged making it public, but Harding feared the political repercussions.

"He did not live to find out how the public would react to the scandals of his administration. In August of 1923, he died in San Francisco of a heart attack."

On November 10, 1958, the Hope Diamond became an official holding of the Smithsonian Institution, where it was put on display for the entire world to enjoy. Whether this succeeded in ending the curse or just in ending the need to fabricate a curse to increase its value and notoriety by fortune-seeking dealers is up for debate.

Chapter 3

The Haunted Octagon

THE OCTAGON HOUSE WAS designed for John Tayloe III by architect William Thornton, the first architect of the United States Capitol. Built between 1799 and 1801, this unusual house was the first house to be completed 'in the neighborhood' of the White House, establishing a beginning point for future development. In today's vernacular, the name Octagon seems an inaccurate name for the six-sided house. During the 18th century, however, the term 'octagon salon' was often used to describe a round room created with eight angled walls, such as the Octagon House entrance hall ... When the president's House, as the White House was known at the time, was destroyed during the War of 1812, James and Dolley Madison accepted John Tayloe's offer to live in the Octagon House temporarily.

—brochure for the Octagon House Museum

Located at 1799 New York Avenue Northwest in the District of Columbia, this National Historic Landmark is the current home of the American Architectural Foundation while also functioning as a museum to enlighten visitors of the building's historic past and architectural legacy. Much attention is paid to the building's design as well as its stint as the temporary residence of the president of the United States. The Treaty of Ghent was signed there in the second-floor parlor on February 17, 1815, thus ending the slightly misnomered War of 1812. But for many visitors the building has another point of interest (which is also highlighted in the museum brochure): "Ghost stories surrounding the tragic deaths at the Octagon House include a strange candle-shaped shadow on the staircase and the faint sound of a falling scream. A somewhat more pleasant ghost, reported to have been seen dancing and enjoying the lilacs, is assumed to be Dolley Madison who adored her temporary stay in the house."

The hauntings at the Octagon all seem to have been related to romantic liaisons, at least three of which seem to have gone tragically wrong.

One of the most striking features of the house is a huge oval staircase.

According to history, Colonel Tayloe and his wife had fifteen children, seven sons and eight daughters, and two of his daughters are believed to still spectrally reside there.

According to legend, sometime prior to the War of 1812 one of the daughters had taken a fancy to a certain British officer whom she began to see on the sly. Given the growing tensions with England (not to overlook the still-open wounds from the American Revolution itself), Tayloe suffered no love loss for the King or his subjects and was not inclined to allow any English officer into his home, let alone one intending to be a suitor for his daughter. Evidently matters came to a head on a dark and stormy night when Tayloe denied his romantically inclined offspring permission to leave for a rendezvous. She supposedly protested loudly and stormed upstairs in furious resignation.

Some accounts say that in her rage her candle became snuffed out and she lost her footing on the stairs, plunging to her death, while others insist she took her own life for either the shame she had brought on her family or the grief of being kept from the man she loved. There is even an account that simply says she tripped—no anger, no grief, just sheer clumsiness.

No matter which account seems most accurate, the outcome is always the same: a scream is heard followed by the thud of her body making contact with the main hall floor. The apparition associated with her is usually seen around the staircase accompanied by a breeze from nowhere that blows out the lantern that now hangs to illuminate the chamber.

It was not long after this occurrence that the Tayloes turned the house over to the Madisons as a temporary executive residence.

When they returned to their home in 1817, Colonel Tayloe was having difficulties with another of his daughters. As the records indicate, he arranged a marriage for her with an eligible and moneyed "landed gentleman," only to have his similarly strong-willed issue elope with a much less desirable match.

It is alleged that the prodigal daughter returned to the Octagon to ask forgiveness and seek her father's blessing for her already consummated marriage. Supposedly she entered the house and went up the same staircase that had claimed her sister's life, only to encounter her stern father at the top. She implored him to talk to her but only met with a steely glare, and in an effort to engage him, she lost her footing, falling backward and breaking her neck as she tumbled down the oval flight of stairs.

Her apparition is usually sighted as a crumpled mass at the foot of the stairs that disappears upon close examination, though a cold spot seems to remain for a time afterward.

Colonel Tayloe was never charged or even suspected of having a hand in the girls' deaths, though modern investigators might have made much of the similar MOs, a pattern of behavior that was recently enough to convict author Michael Peterson of the so-called "Staircase Murders."

A more recent morbid tale of a lovelorn ghost tied to the house was included in *Washington Revisited—The Ghostlore of the Nation's Capital* by John Alexander. Alexander writes:

"Reporters have frequently filed stories about screams of agony, sobs, and moans of despair, echoing through the Octagon. A writer in the later part of the 1800s said 'the spectral goings on there are so extraordinary that no one will live in the house.' The article attributed the moans and sobs to a slave who had been whipped or otherwise tortured to death by some former proprietor. . . .

"In 1902 the American Institute of Architects acquired the Octagon. Almost a half-century of deterioration was stopped. Restoration work was begun. One day as workmen were repairing a wall they may have inadvertently solved the riddle of those 'thumping sounds' that plagued residents for years. They came upon a skeleton of a young woman. Her finger bones on both hands were clenched tight, as though she had died knocking on the wall. She was taken out of the wall and given a proper burial. The thumping sounds were never again heard in that part of the house.

"At the time, one of the Colonel's descendants said that she seemed to recall a tale her grandmother had told of a soldier and a slave girl when the French Ministry occupied the Octagon. They were lovers, but in a jealous rage, the soldier killed her, and somehow managed to seal her body inside a hollow wall."

Still, notwithstanding these forlorn phantoms of past passions unknown, the most famous specter of the Octagon House is undoubtedly the spouse of the fourth president of the United States, Dolley Payne Todd Madison.

Born in 1768, this archetypal First Lady was previously married to John Todd Jr., a Philadelphia lawyer with whom she had two sons,

John Payne and William Temple. Unfortunately, in 1793 a yellow fever epidemic swept through Philadelphia, claiming the lives of her husband and son William within weeks of each other.

In May 1794, widow Dolley was introduced to her future husband, Representative James Madison of Virginia (the so-called architect of the U.S. Constitution) by her friend Senator Aaron Burr of New York (the soon-to-be vice president and infamous duelist who killed Alexander Hamilton). Dolley had come to know and befriend Burr when he was a boarder at her mother's rooming house. Though Madison was seventeen years her senior (Burr was only twelve years older than her), they began a courtship, and on September 15, 1794, James, age forty-three, and Dolley, twenty-six, were married.

In addition to being a popular Washington hostess, Dolley is also remembered for valor at the White House during the War of 1812. In her own words from her correspondence dated August 23, 1814:

MY HUSBAND LEFT ME yesterday morning to join General Winder. He inquired anxiously whether I had courage or firmness to remain in the President's house until his return on the morrow, or succeeding day, and on my assurance that I had no fear but for him, and the success of our army, he left, beseeching me to take care of myself, and of the Cabinet papers, public and private. I have since received two dispatches from him, written with a pencil. The last is alarming, because he desires I should be ready at a moment's warning to enter my carriage, and leave the city; that the enemy seemed stronger than had at first been reported, and it might happen that they would reach the city with the intention of destroying it. I am accordingly ready; I have pressed as many Cabinet papers into trunks as to fill one carriage; our private property must be sacrificed, as it is impossible to procure wagons for its transportation. I am determined not to go myself until I see Mr. Madison safe, so that he can accompany me, as I hear of much hostility towards him. Disaffection stalks around us. My friends and acquaintances are all gone, even Colonel C. with his hundred, who were stationed as a guard in this enclosure. French John (a faithful servant), with his usual activity and resolution, offers to spike the cannon at the gate, and lay a train of powder, which would blow up the British, should they enter the house. To the last proposition I positively object, without being able to make him understand why all advantages in war may not be taken.

Wednesday Morning, twelve o'clock.—Since sunrise I have been turning my spy-glass in every direction, and watching with un-wearied anxiety, hoping to discover the approach of my dear husband and his friends; but, alas! I can descry only groups of military, wandering in all directions, as if there was a lack of arms, or of spirit to fight for their own fireside.

Three o'clock.—Will you believe it, my sister? we have had a battle, or skirmish, near Bladensburg, and here I am still, within sound of the cannon! Mr. Madison comes not. May God protect us! Two messengers, covered with dust, come to bid me fly; but here I mean to wait for him. . . . At this late hour a wagon has been procured, and I have had it filled with plate and the most valuable portable articles, belonging to the house. Whether it will reach its destination, the "Bank of Maryland," or fall into the hands of British soldiery, events must determine. Our kind friend, Mr. Carroll, has come to hasten my departure, and in a very bad humor with me, because I insist on waiting until the large picture of General Washington is secured, and it requires to be unscrewed from the wall. This process was found too tedious for these perilous moments; I have ordered the frame to be broken, and the canvas taken out. It is done! and the precious portrait placed in the hands of two gentlemen of New York, for safe keeping. And now, dear sister, I must leave this house, or the retreating army will make me a prisoner in it by filling up the road I am directed to take. When I shall again write to you, or where I shall be to-morrow, I cannot tell!

As history has recorded, Dolley left the White House with all she could carry moments before the British arrived, leaving an uneaten dinner on the table. The soldiers ate the meal and burned the White House to the ground.

It was due to this circumstance that the Madisons accepted Colonel Tayloe's offer and made the Octagon House the temporary president's residence. From September 1814 to October 1815 the Octagon functioned as the president's house/executive residence. The popular First Lady had no intention of cutting back on the presidential social schedule and immediately set up almost daily affairs in their new residence where she showed off the latest fashions while currying favor for her husband's administration.

Over the years there have been numerous apparitions associated with this singular First Lady. Initially several inhabitants of the Octagon in later years noticed what appeared to be a turbaned woman dressed in Eastern garb leaning up against the mantelpiece in the main ballroom of the house. One newspaper article from the latter part of the century called attention to the "turbaned wispy form of a woman" who danced through the entrance. This initially threw off researchers into the identity of this figure until it was brought to their attention that Dolley Madison, who was short of stature for even her time, was exceptionally self-conscious of her height and as a result often tended toward exotic fashions while entertaining, including, usually, a feathered turban of some kind that would help disguise her true height. Further inquiry revealed that it was by that exact ballroom mantelpiece that Dolley used to station herself to greet her guests before whisking herself out onto to the dance floor to enjoy the gaiety of the affair.

During her stay at the Octagon, the First Lady used its proximity to the White House site to keep tabs on the construction plans for the new executive residence and in particular a restoration of the gardens that she had taken pride in designing.

In addition to the 1600 Pennsylvania rose garden, which she made sure to preserve after the conflagration, Dolley also was quite fond of tending her patches of lilacs, some of which she added to the garden at the Octagon as she frequently, fragrantly augmented her distinctive fashionable look with more than a hint of lilac scent. Ergo, it is not surprising that several of the spectral apparitions have also been associated with the lingering scent of lilacs once the visual component of the apparition has disappeared.

Indeed, one of the lilac-scented alleged Dolley sightings at the Octagon hints at a scandalous assignation. More than one visitor to the building has claimed to have seen the turbaned phantom female apparently in full party mode dabbing herself with lilac water only to have the figure move as if summoned to the garden doors, at which point she disappeared and then reappeared later, adjusting her outfit self-consciously.

This apparition dovetails nicely with the tale of a surprise visitor to the Octagon garden during one of Dolley's parties while her husband, the president, was away. This surprise visitor who scaled the back garden wall so as to venture onto the premises unseen was none other than the out-of-favor former vice president, duelist, and possible "enemy of the United States," Aaron Burr, who had been keeping a low profile since his 1807 trial for treason. (Burr had even spent several years prior to the War of 1812 living in sort of an exile in Europe before returning to the United States under his mother's maiden name of Edwards.) More than just the man who introduced her to her second husband, Burr may also have been a prior suitor to the widow Dolley some twenty years before. The two may have kept in touch, and oral accounts of the First Lady's social life tend to imply that a certain amount of "affection" still existed between the two of them.

Whether this apparition is also a case of spectral assignation is unknown, though for many the visual accounts of the scene do tend to suggest scandal with just a hint of lilacs.

It would appear that this First Lady is more than willing to do double (if not triple) duty on the haunting circuit. After the Madisons left the president's residence for a townhouse on Nineteenth Street, Dolley settled on the place as her final home and indeed after her death was occasionally seen in a rocking chair out front as she was in her later years, often smiling at observant passersby.

Even in her postdeath retirement, she still kept a watchful eye on the White House and the garden she had designed as a legacy for future First Ladies. According to White House usher Gary Walters, there is a popular legend of Dolley Madison coming back to 1600 Pennsylvania Avenue during the Wilson administration when Mrs. Wilson wanted the rose garden dug up. Dolley's ghost supposedly arrived and told them not to disturb her garden. The seminal White House hostess got her way, and the flower beds were protected . . . and rumor has it that she still makes an occasional appearance to make sure things remain that way.

Chapter 4

The First Ladies' Haunted Homes

One doesn't have to reach back to the days of Dolley Madison and Mary Todd Lincoln to hear rumors of First Ladies and hauntings.

According to a 1976 article in the *National Enquirer*, soon-to-be-president Jimmy Carter and his wife, Rosalynn, actually lived in a haunted house for a while. In the words of the soon-to-be First Lady: "I knew that the house was haunted ever since I was a little girl, because I grew up in the town. . . . I used to go all the way through the woods to avoid walking close to it. When I did go near it, I saw flashing lights in the attic when there was nobody in the house."

According to the *Enquirer*, the Carters lived in the haunted residence from 1954 to 1959. Located just outside of Plains, Georgia, the residence, built in 1850, was an old wood-frame plantation-style building that was supposedly haunted by the spirits of some Civil War–era Union soldiers who were killed there.

"I never saw any ghosts—I don't believe in them—but I heard something in the attic every night that sent shivers up my spine. Those eerie noises gave me goosebumps. One day while my son was playing he found two loose bricks in the attic fireplace. When he picked up the bricks, he discovered a room beneath the fireplace, four feet deep and six feet wide. There was nothing in the room but a chair."

According to a later article in the *Examiner* (another tabloid) Rosalynn Carter also recalled stories she heard of a tiny, silent white dog that was said to appear on the front steps. It always suddenly vanished when someone reached down to pat it, though the original *Enquirer* article actually ascribes this assertion to the home's previous owner, a Georgia doctor.

(Author's note: The *Examiner* article, which ran in 1983, after the Carters had already vacated 1600 Pennsylvania Avenue, also included a photo with the following caption: "Ex–First Lady Rosalynn Carter inspects secret space above the hearth in attic of wood framed haunted house [top] in Plains, Georgia," and the photo does indeed feature a woman who could be and/or resembles the former First Lady.)

Similarly, when it was announced that former First Lady Hillary Clinton would be purchasing a D.C. apartment for use during her senatorial days away from home in Chappaqua, New York, numerous occult enthusiasts noted that the three-story redbrick Georgian house at 3067 Whitehaven Street, built in 1951 with seven and a half baths, a fireplace, heated pool, spacious backyard, slate-floored foyer, and solid cherry wood spiral staircase that leads to the second floor was in an area of the district that has become affectionately known among the paranormal set as Spookville.

According to an article titled "Hillary's Haunted Neighborhood," the natives of the area prior to the European invasion in the seventeenth century had used this area as an ossuary (burial grounds) for their dead chiefs and shaman.

In addition to this clichéd "haunted Indian burial ground," the neighborhood also includes the aforementioned Octagon House and the Woodrow Wilson house, where, according to paranormal expert Hans Holzer, the spirit of the so-called Peace President has vowed to return and make his presence known once a new world order has been established.

Perhaps the rise in prominence of Hillary Clinton in both the government and the neighborhood is exactly what he has been waiting for.

The Curse of Tecumseh

Consider the following set of possibly related events:

1840 William Henry Harrison elected president of
the United States

On the dreary and damp wintry day of his inauguration, Harrison refused to bundle up and caught a cold. Without any real time to rest or recover (due to numerous petitioners who arrived at the White House to cash in certain favors that were promised on the campaign trail) the cold turned into pneumonia and the newly elected ninth president of the United States died a month later.

1860 Abraham Lincoln elected president, then
reelected four years later

On April 14, 1865, the Civil War finally over, Lincoln and his wife decided to go to the theater for an evening of light comedy. They chose *Our American Cousin* at Ford's Theater and were enjoying the show when Confederate sympathizer John Wilkes Booth burst into their box and shot the president point-blank in the back of the head, then made his escape. The sixteenth president of the United States died early the following morning.

1880 James A. Garfield elected president

On July 2, 1881, en route to his college alma mater, Garfield was shot twice at fairly close range by Charles J. Guiteaua, a disappointed federal job seeker and stalwart supporter of then–vice president Chester Arthur. Neither shot was necessarily fatal, though both (and their subsequent surgical treatments) led to numerous infections and the overall weakening of the constitution of the twentieth U.S. president . . . and three months later, despite an extended period of convalescence, he died of complications from blood poisoning and pneumonia, two months shy of his fiftieth birthday.

1900 William McKinley elected president

On September 6, 1901, while attending the Pan-American Exposition in Buffalo, New York, McKinley was shot twice by anarchist Leon Frank Czolgosz, and eight days later the twenty-fifth president died from complications from his wounds, attributed to gangrene.

1920 Warren G. Harding elected president

On August 2, 1923, Harding, the twenty-ninth president, his administration disgraced and wracked with scandals (such as the Teapot Dome affair) died of what the papers referred to as "a stroke of apoplexy" (though it was probably a heart attack) approximately two and a half years after taking office.

1940 Franklin D. Roosevelt elected president, his third term in office

Roosevelt, the thirty-second president, though long plagued with illness and a weakening of his general constitution compounded by polio and the demands on him as an Allied leader during World War II, died of natural causes on April 12,

1945, less than four months after taking the oath of office for a fourth term.

1960 John F. Kennedy elected president
On a trip to Dallas on November 22, 1963, while riding in a carefully guarded open car, Kennedy was shot by a gunman (believed to be Lee Harvey Oswald, who was later apprehended and killed in custody by Jack Ruby, a man with known mob ties). The thirty-fifth president was pronounced dead approximately a half hour later.

What Do They Have in Common?

Every twenty years, from 1840 to 1960, the man elected president died in office.

The causes of death were as different as the timings of the mortal event (sometimes close to initial election, sometimes much later and not even during the same term, for that matter), but nonetheless a recognizable pattern seems to have emerged.

This pattern was initially recognized in 1931 by Robert Ripley in his famous comic strip column *Believe It or Not!* and became known by a variety of names including the Presidential Curse, the Twenty-Year Curse, and the Zero-Year Curse. With the later continuation of this pattern through the Roosevelt and Kennedy tenures in office, Washington reporters such as Jack Anderson would often interject the subject into their questioning of candidates during zero-year elections. (While campaigning for reelection in 1980, Jimmy Carter, the thirty-ninth president, memorably responded to such an inquiry by saying "I'm not afraid. If I knew it was going to happen, I would go ahead and be president and do the best I could, for the last day I could.")

Lacking anything more than this pattern of events, some historians have decided to trace it back to its origins—namely the election of William Henry Harrison, the man who still holds the record for the shortest term in office for a duly elected U.S. president. Despite the brevity of his term in office, his official White House biography reads as follows:

"GIVE HIM A BARREL of hard cider and settle a pension of two thousand a year on him, and my word for it," a Democratic newspaper foolishly gibed, "he will sit . . . by the side of a 'sea coal' fire, and study moral philosophy." The Whigs, seizing on this political misstep, in 1840 presented their candidate William Henry Harrison as a simple frontier Indian fighter, living in a log cabin and drinking cider, in sharp contrast to an aristocratic champagne-sipping Van Buren.

Harrison was in fact a scion of the Virginia planter aristocracy. He was born at Berkeley in 1773. He studied classics and history at Hampden-Sydney College, then began the study of medicine in Richmond.

Suddenly, that same year, 1791, Harrison switched interests. He obtained a commission as ensign in the First Infantry of the Regular Army, and headed to the Northwest, where he spent much of his life.

In the campaign against the Indians, Harrison served as aide-de-camp to General "Mad Anthony" Wayne at the Battle of Fallen Timbers, which opened most of the Ohio area to settlement. After resigning from the Army in 1798, he became Secretary of the Northwest Territory, was its first delegate to Congress, and helped obtain legislation dividing the Territory into the Northwest and Indiana Territories. In 1801 he became Governor of the Indiana Territory, serving 12 years.

His prime task as governor was to obtain title to Indian lands so settlers could press forward into the wilderness. When the Indians retaliated, Harrison was responsible for defending the settlements.

The threat against settlers became serious in 1809. An eloquent and energetic chieftain, Tecumseh, with his religious brother, the Prophet, began to strengthen an Indian confederation to prevent further encroachment. In 1811 Harrison received permission to attack the confederacy.

While Tecumseh was away seeking more allies, Harrison led about a thousand men toward the Prophet's town. Suddenly, before dawn on November 7, the Indians attacked his camp on Tippecanoe River. After heavy fighting, Harrison repulsed them, but suffered 190 dead and wounded.

The Battle of Tippecanoe, upon which Harrison's fame was to rest, disrupted Tecumseh's confederacy but failed to diminish Indian raids. By the spring of 1812, they were again terrorizing the frontier.

In the War of 1812 Harrison won more military laurels when he was given the command of the Army in the Northwest with the rank of brigadier general. At the Battle of the Thames, north of Lake Erie, on October 5, 1813, he defeated the combined British and Indian forces, and killed Tecumseh. The Indians scattered, never again to offer serious resistance in what was then called the Northwest.

Thereafter Harrison returned to civilian life; the Whigs, in need of a national hero, nominated him for President in 1840. He won by a majority of less than 150,000, but swept the Electoral College, 234 to 60.

When he arrived in Washington in February 1841, Harrison let Daniel Webster edit his Inaugural Address, ornate with classical allusions. Webster obtained some deletions, boasting in a jolly fashion that he had killed "seventeen Roman proconsuls as dead as smelts, every one of them."

Webster had reason to be pleased, for while Harrison was nationalistic in his outlook, he emphasized in his Inaugural that he would be obedient to the will of the people as expressed through Congress.

But before he had been in office a month, he caught a cold that developed into pneumonia. On April 4, 1841, he died—the first President to die in office—and with him died the Whig program.

Given the long-standing interest in the so-called Indian Prophecy of George Washington (as related in the first chapter), an informal consensus developed in the paranormal community that began to ascribe the origin of the curse to an encounter during Harrison's Indian fighting days, leading to the curse to be renamed the Curse of Tecumseh or the Curse of Tippecanoe.

Now, being completely candid, the White House biography of Harrison does downplay his role in the organized genocide strategy that was a definite part of "his prime task . . . to obtain title to Indian lands so settlers could press forward into the wilderness," and indeed latter-day historians tend to side with Tecumseh and his shaman brother Tenskwatawa as merely honorably defending their people, the Shawnee tribe of the Mississippi Valley, from the military-fronted interlopers from the East Coast.

Encarta encyclopedia's partial biography of the Indian leader reads as follows (italics have been added for emphasis):

"Tecumseh (1768?–1813), Shawnee leader, who fought against United States expansion into the Midwest in the early 19th century. Born in what is now Ohio, he was the son of a Shawnee chief who was killed fighting white settlers in the Battle of Point Pleasant (1774). In 1794 Tecumseh took part in the Battle of Fallen Timbers, in which a coalition of tribes was defeated by the U.S. general Anthony Wayne. *Tecumseh became known for his opposition to any surrender of Native American land to whites, holding that a cession of land by any one tribe was illegal without the consent of all the others. He and his brother Tenskwatawa, a religious visionary known as The Prophet, preached against Native American adoption of white customs—especially the use of liquor. In 1808 they were forced out of Ohio and moved to Indiana, where they tried to form a broad alliance of Native American tribes with help from the British in Canada.* Their plans were thwarted when Tenskwatawa was defeated by U.S. forces under William Henry Harrison at the Battle of Tippecanoe in 1811. Tecumseh fought on the British side in the War of 1812 and was killed in the Battle of the Thames, near Thamesville, Ontario, on October 5, 1813."

His brother's bio also reads as follows:

"Shawnee Prophet (1775?–1837?), Native North American of the Shawnee tribe; brother of Tecumseh. His Native American name was Tenskwatawa. He announced himself as a prophet bearing a revelation from the Native American master of life. The message urged the renunciation of the acquired ways of the whites and the return to Native American modes and customs in all matters. His doctrines were widespread among Native Americans, and his prestige was enhanced when he foretold a solar eclipse in 1806. His influence gave rise to the plan to confederate all the Native Americans in opposition to the whites— a plan that inspired the Creek War of 1813. In 1811 he led the Native American forces in the battle of Tippecanoe. The movement inspired by him provided many recruits for the British in the War of 1812, after which Tenskwatawa retired to Canada with a British pension. He returned to Ohio in 1826 and accompanied his people to Missouri and farther west into Kansas, where he died."

Both Indian leaders now come across as far more civilized than their white conquerors of the time. As several oral histories seem to indicate, General Harrison was less than honorable in his treatment of the native residents and practiced a policy of slaughtering undefended innocents in any villages he came upon. His defensive forces crippled, Tecumseh had little option but to release all prisoners he had captured during his defensive campaign, recognizing that he had little power in *this* world to extract his people's rightful revenge on the barbarian conqueror who would eventually become president.

As the legend now relates, Tecumseh is supposed to have released prisoners, with a prophetic message for the leader of the U.S. troops, General Harrison. "Harrison will die in his office. . . . I who caused the Sun to darken and Red Men to give up firewater tell you Harrison will die. And after him, every Great Chief chosen every 20 years thereafter will die. And when each one dies, let everyone remember the death of our people."

A different version of the story attributes the curse to Tenskwatawa, at that point a Shawnee medicine man also known as the Prophet, twenty years later. His curse was revenge for the death of his half brother Tecumseh, who died in the 1813 Battle of the Thames fighting against U.S. troops again led by Harrison. As this version tells it, the Prophet was having his portrait painted in the presence of several politicians when he heard that his old nemesis would soon be an enviable candidate for the presidency. His angry response was: "Harrison will die I tell you, and after him, every Great Chief chosen every 20 years thereafter will die. And when each one dies, let everyone remember the death of my people."

It is noteworthy that these origins of the curse seemed to surface only after the nation's shaming of itself in the 1960s and 1970s over its treatment of the native Americans and that there is virtually no contemporaneous documentation related to the curse in the nineteenth century. Its sins of the fathers bringing to bear punishment on future generations may be poetic but also seems far less than credible.

Still there is that nagging pattern of death that seemed to continue even after it was initially noticed in 1931, but there are probably several other possible paranormal causes beyond the so-called Tippecanoe Curse.

An article by Jesse Valdez cites a theory that attributes the pattern of events to the stars, contending, "Many astrologers claim that the alignment of Jupiter and Saturn may have an effect over the 20-year pattern of presidential deaths (Jupiter representing optimism, expansion and the ruler, while Saturn symbolizing death, pessimism, and contraction). Alignments under the earth signs (Taurus, Capricorn and Virgo) have resulted in death to every president in office . . . however, the one alignment under an air sign, Libra (in 1980), seemingly allowed President Reagan to avert death."

This of course does bring up the "curse busting" case of the fortieth president, Ronald Reagan, who was elected in 1980 but did manage to serve out both of his terms. However, almost two months after taking office, Reagan was shot and wounded by a deranged would-be assassin named John F. Hinckley, who had hoped to win the affections of actress Jodie Foster by his deed. The quick attention of the Secret Service followed by the expert attention of a crack medical team assured the president's survival and well-being (he was even able to quip to his wife that he "forgot to duck").

It would not be inappropriate to point out that Reagan's wounds were no less serious than those that eventually lead to Garfield's death, but the advances of modern medicine provided a marked decrease in the mortality risk and indeed might have been the type of outside factor that thwarted the nineteenth-century curse. Others who might be seen as biased or as being non-Reagan fans have also pointed out that the fortieth president was already suffering from Alzheimer's disease when he left office, and that perhaps the curse was manifesting itself as a sort of brain death.

Other curse debunkers also bring up the case of George W. Bush, the forty-third president of the United States, who was elected in 2000 and managed to serve out his presidency mortally unscathed. Others point out that there is considerable debate over whether Bush was indeed *elected* president (as opposed to *selected* by the Supreme Court in its landmark decision *Bush v. Gore*), given all the controversy surrounding the 2000 election.

I guess we will have to wait around to see who is elected in 2020 and how he or she fares before we can be assured that the curse has been lifted once and for all.

The Kennedy-Lincoln
Connection

Within weeks of John F. Kennedy's death, various students of cosmic conspiracy theories began deconstructing his and Lincoln's assassinations, calling attention to the similarities between the two occurrences.

Some have suggested that there is some sort of cosmic connection between the two events, while others (like the urban-myth debunking team at Snopes.com) dismiss any significance of the coincidences at hand and indeed have tried to place them in a constructed statistical context that further waters down the singularity of each coincidence.

Still, when Vincent Bugliosi put together his mammoth work on that infamous day in Dallas and its aftermath (*Reclaiming History: The Assassination of President John F. Kennedy*) he considered it necessary to include a section on the "connections" between the two events.

The coincidences can be grouped into thematically linked subsections that break down as follows: "100 Years Apart," "The Wives," "The Alleged Assassins," "The Deaths," and "Letters in the Names." I've also included a few other coincidences that have usually been included in such compilations but have no validity whatsoever.

The bottom line is that there are indeed an awful lot of coincidences, but whether there is some sort of occult connection between the two still remains to be proven.

100 Years Apart

- Both Lincoln and Kennedy had served in the U.S. House of Representatives: Lincoln elected in 1846, Kennedy in 1946.
- Both Lincoln and Kennedy were elected president after each had unsuccessfully sought to get the vice presidential nomination of their party: Lincoln in 1856, Kennedy in 1956.
- Lincoln was elected in 1860, Kennedy in 1960.
- The man Lincoln defeated to become president, Stephen Douglas, was born in 1813. The man Kennedy defeated to become president, Richard Nixon, was born in 1913.
- Lincoln's successor, Andrew Johnson, was born in 1808, and Kennedy's successor, Lyndon Johnson, was born in 1908.

The Wives

- Lincoln and Kennedy, while in their thirties, each married a pretty, sophisticated twenty-four-year-old brunette who spoke French fluently.
- Both wives lost a child while in residence at the White House.
- Both presidents were in the company of their wives when they were shot; each wife cradled her husband's head in her lap after the deed.

The Alleged Assassins

- Both assassins were known by their three names: John Wilkes Booth and Lee Harvey Oswald.
- Both assassins were southerners who held extremist views.

- Both assassins were murdered before they could be brought to trial.
- Booth shot Lincoln in a theater and fled to a warehouse; Oswald shot Kennedy from a warehouse and fled to a theater (a slight stretch depending on your definition of warehouse).

The Deaths

- Both men were assassinated in the presence of their wives.
- Each man was killed by a bullet that entered the head from behind.
- Though both were shot in the head, which normally causes immediate death, neither died instantly.
- Lincoln was killed in Ford's Theater. Kennedy met his death while riding in a Lincoln convertible made by the Ford Motor Company.
- Both Lincoln and Kennedy died on a Friday.
- A Lincoln staffer, Miss Kennedy, told him not to go to the theater. A Kennedy staffer, Miss Lincoln, told him not to go to Dallas.

Letters in the Names

- *Lincoln* and *Kennedy* each have seven letters.
- *Andrew Johnson* and *Lyndon Johnson* each have thirteen letters.
- *John Wilkes Booth* and *Lee Harvey Oswald* each have fifteen letters.

Easily refuted coincidences (usually included on this list) that are factually inaccurate or just plain stupid

- The name of Lincoln's private secretary was Kennedy, while the name of Kennedy's private secretary was Lincoln. (Kennedy did have a secretary named Lincoln, but there is no record of Lincoln having one named Kennedy.)
- John Wilkes Booth was born in 1839; Lee Harvey Oswald was born in 1939, one hundred years later. (Booth was actually born in 1838.)
- A week before Lincoln was shot, he was in Monroe, Maryland; a week before Kennedy was shot, he was in Marilyn Monroe. (Marilyn Monroe died more than a year before Kennedy was shot.)

The Secret Societies
of the Founding Fathers

Millions of fans have been waiting in earnest for Dan Brown's follow-up to *The Da Vinci Code*, and those who were paying close attention to his deposition in a recent court case in England were given a treat as he revealed a few clues about his upcoming thriller, tentatively titled *The Solomon Key*.

"I started looking into the Illuminati, and what I found was material for a great thriller. I read conspiracy theories on the Illuminati that included infiltration of the British Parliament and U.S. Treasury, secret involvement with the Masons, affiliation with covert satanic cults, a plan for a New World Order . . . for example, the design of the Great Seal on the U.S. dollar bill includes an illustration of a pyramid—an object which arguably has nothing to do with American history. . . .

"I have asked myself why all this clandestine material interests me. At a fundamental level my interest in secret societies came from growing up in New England, surrounded by the clandestine clubs of Ivy League universities, the Masonic lodges of the Founding Fathers, and the hidden hallways of early government power. I see New England as having a long tradition of elite private clubs, fraternities, and secrecy—indeed, my third Robert Langdon novel (a work in progress) is set within the Masons. I have always found the concept of secret societies, codes, and means of communication fascinating. In my youth

I was very aware of the Skull & Bones club at Yale. I had good friends who were members of Harvard's secret 'finals' clubs. In the town where I grew up, there was a Masonic lodge, and nobody could (or would) tell me what happened behind those closed doors. All of this secrecy captivated me as a young man."

Indeed, as in the recent and highly incredulous box-office success of the *National Treasure* series, starring Nicolas Cage, the secrets of the founding fathers are more than fertile fodder for fictioners of all genres.

Noted fantasy author Katherine Kurtz assayed an alternate version of the American Revolution in her novel *Two Crowns for America,* where, quoting from her historical afterword, "Jacobite exiles . . . became inextricably intertwined in the shaping of the New Order that was to become the United States of America, and the thread of Freemasonry that bound them to the American cause, and the Unknown Master (Author's note: The Unknown Master is believed to be the mystic the Comte de Saint Germaine, an actual historic person.) believed to have directed much of their activity from the other side of the Atlantic—toward what ultimate end, we can only guess. . . . Exactly how Jacobite kings and Crowns and the thread of Freemasonry actually did figure in the eventual birth of the American Republic probably will never be known for certain. . . ."

Similarly, legal thriller author Brad Meltzer spun a contemporary Washington, D.C.–based thriller that drew on some of the secrets of the founders in his *Book of Fate* where, in the words of *Booklist's* favorable review, "[The protagonist] must decipher a two-century-old code and penetrate the secrets of Masonic history." (The code mentioned is a specific form of shorthand used by Thomas Jefferson to grade his officers in a manner that would enable him to take notes in their presence without their discerning his true opinions of them and the matters at hand; this was just one of Jefferson's many creative innovations and has nothing to do with the paranormal at all.)

But fiction aside, there is more than a touch of the occult in the affairs of the founding fathers, and indeed a passed-on legacy of "secret societies" that to this day occasionally raises its head in the open media (e.g., the attention focused on Yale's Skull & Bones society when it was observed that both the 2004 presidential candidates were members: Republican George W. Bush and Democrat John Kerry).

However, even among secret societies, some are more secret than others. Take, for example, the Hellfire Club, which was founded by Sir Francis Dashwood in the eighteenth century in England under the more acceptable moniker of the Friars of St. Francis. The group included among its secret membership a certain Brother Benjamin of Cookham, or as he was better known in the soon-to-be United States, Benjamin Franklin. In essence, this was more of a hedonism club than an actual secret society, but Dashwood included among its ritual regalia elements he had amassed from several other secret societies, including the Rosicrucians and the Freemasons.

This of course leads us to the matters of the Rosicrucians and the Masons. A Rosicrucian is defined as a member of an international organization (the Ancient Mystic Order Rosae Crucis and the Rosicrucian Order) formed in the seventeenth and eighteenth centuries devoted to the study of ancient mystical, philosophical, and religious doctrines and concerned with the application of these doctrines to modern life. This secretive order has also been linked to so-called conspiracies to initiate a new world order of one government and has included in its membership such men as Thomas Paine, Ben Franklin, and George Washington (and possibly Thomas Jefferson, whose open-mindedness and worldview on numerous subjects would have made him a natural member, and his years in France as an ambassador undoubtedly would have put him in contact with several senior members of the order). But for the most part this organization has not yielded any evidence of wrongdoing, manipulation, or political puppeteering, at least in the United States.

The same, however, cannot be said for the other notable secret society, namely the Masons ... at least according to the amount of attention that has been focused on this group vis-à-vis their relationship with the founding fathers and subsequent U.S. presidents.

Consider the following:

Nine of the original fifty-six signers of the Declaration of Independence were high-level Masons (William Ellery, Benjamin Franklin, John Hancock, Joseph Hewes, William Hooper, Robert Treat Paine, Richard Stockton, George Walton, and William Whipple).

Thirteen of the original forty signers of the Constitution were high-level Masons (Gunning Bedford Jr., John Blair, David Brearley, Jacob Broom, Daniel Carroll, Jonathan Dayton, John Dickinson, Benjamin Franklin, Nicholas Gilman, Rufus King, James McHenry, William Patterson, and George Washington).

And fifteen of our forty-three presidents have been Masons, with their Masonic histories indisputably documented as follows:

1. *George Washington, first president, 1789–1797, commanding general during the American Revolution, made a Mason August 4, 1753, in Fredericksburg Lodge (now No. 4), A.F. & A.M., Fredericksburg, Virginia.*

2. *James Monroe, fifth president, 1817–1825, made a Mason November 9, 1775, in Williamsburg Lodge (now No. 6), A.F. & A.M., Williamsburg, Virginia.*

3. *Andrew Jackson, seventh president, 1829–1837, Harmony Lodge No. 1, Nashville, Tennessee, an honorary member of Federal Lodge No. 1, F. & A.M., Washington, D.C., and Jackson Lodge No. 1, F. & A.M., Tallahassee, Florida. In 1822 and 1823 he served as the grand master of Masons in Tennessee.*

4. *James Knox Polk, eleventh president, 1845–1849, made a Mason September 4, 1820, in Columbia Lodge No. 31, F. & A.M., Columbia, Tennessee.*

5. *James Buchanan, fifteenth president, 1857–1861, made a Mason January 24, 1817, in Lodge No. 43, F. & A.M., Lancaster, Pennsylvania.*

6. *Andrew Johnson, seventeenth president, 1865–1869, made a Mason in May 1851, in Greeneville Lodge No. 119 (now No. 3), F. & A.M., Greeneville, Tennessee.*

7. *James Abram Garfield, twentieth president, 1881, made a Mason November 22, 1864, in Columbus Lodge No. 30, F. & A.M., Columbus, Ohio.*

8. *William McKinley, twenty-fifth president, 1897–1901, made a Mason May 3, 1865, in Hiram Lodge No. 21, A.F. & A.M., Winchester, Virginia.*

9. *Theodore Roosevelt, twenty-sixth president, 1901–1909, made a Mason April 24, 1901, in Matinecock Lodge No. 806, F. & A.M., Oyster Bay, New York.*

10. *William Howard Taft, twenty-seventh president, 1909–1913, made a Mason at Sight in an "occasional Lodge called for that purpose" on February 18, 1909, in the Scottish Rite Cathedral, Cincinnati, Ohio, by Charles S. Hoskinson, grand master of Masons in Ohio.*

11. *Warren Gamaliel Harding, twenty-ninth president, 1921–1923, made a Mason August 27, 1920, in Marion Lodge No. 70, F. & A.M., Marion, Ohio.*

12. *Franklin Delano Roosevelt, thirty-second president, 1933–1945, made a Mason November 28, 1911, in Holland Lodge No. 8, F. & A.M., New York, New York, where George Washington held honorary membership.*

13. *Harry S Truman, thirty-third president, 1945–1951, made a Mason March 18, 1909, in Belton Lodge No. 450, A.F. & A.M., Belton, Missouri. He served as the grand master of Masons of Missouri in 1940. Initiated: February 9, 1909, Belton Lodge No. 450, Belton, Missouri.*

At the annual session of the Grand Lodge of Missouri, September 24–25, 1940, Truman was elected (by a landslide) the ninety-seventh grand master of Masons of Missouri and served until October 1, 1941. Truman was made a sovereign grand inspector general, 33°, and honorary member of the Supreme Council on October 19, 1945 at the Supreme Council A.A.S.R. Southern Jurisdiction Headquarters in Washington, D.C. He was also elected an honorary grand master of the International Supreme Council, Order of DeMolay. (On May 18, 1959, Truman received a fifty-year award, the only U.S. president to reach that golden anniversary in Freemasonry.)

14. *Lyndon Baines Johnson, thirty-sixth president, 1963–1969. Entered as Apprentice Degree, Johnson City Lodge No. 561, Johnson City, Texas, October 30, 1937.*

15. *Gerald R. Ford Jr., thirty-eighth president, 1974–1977. He was raised to the Sublime Degree of Master Mason on May 18, 1951,*

in Columbia Lodge No. 3, F. & A.M., of Washington, D.C., as a
courtesy for Malta Lodge No. 465, F. & A.M., of Grand Rapids,
Michigan.

In the general media, such lists are usually followed by hints of mysticism and mentions of the integration of Masonic symbols into the fabric (organizational structure, city grid, currency, etc.) of the original government as set up by the founding fathers. It is also usually brought up that George Washington was sworn into office using a "Masonic" Bible, though this is widely taken out of context. Actually, the "inaugural" inaugural suffered from a lack of attention to detail during its planning, resulting in no one having a Bible at hand for the swearing-in ceremony. The quick-thinking New York chancellor who was officiating immediately recalled that there would be one available at Saint John's Masonic Lodge, which was in the vicinity, and dispatched an aide to borrow it.

But who are the Masons and what do they believe?
Well, according to a press release from one of their current chapters:

"Freemasonry is the world's first and largest fraternal organization. It is based on the belief that each man can make a difference in the world. There are approximately 5 million Masons worldwide, including 2 million in the United States. The organization dates back to the guilds of European stonemasons who built castles and cathedrals during the Middle Ages. Temporary buildings called lodges were built next to the cathedrals, and the Masons used them to meet, receive their pay, plan their work, train new apprentices, and socialize. The first Grand Lodge was established in England in 1717; by 1731, Masonry had spread to the American colonies. Benjamin Franklin, George Washington, Paul Revere, and other founding fathers were among the first Masons in the United States."

And when asked what their mission/objective is . . .

"The mission of Freemasonry is brotherhood, community involvement, and self-improvement through education, family values, moral standards, and charity."

. . . which all sounds pretty harmless and nonconspiratorial.

Yet many critics today (especially those affiliated with extreme factions of the evangelical movement) point out that the Masons were largely responsible for the increased secularism in France as early as the era of the Revolution and indeed have continued to promote secular education through political reform, recognizing the rights of non-Christians and atheists.

These same critics also highlight the pervasive yet subtly integrated Masonic symbology throughout U.S. iconography.

Case in point: the overall design of Washington, D.C.

As Brad Meltzer synopsized in his author's note in *The Book of Fate*, "Jefferson, Washington, and architect Pierre Charles L'Enfant, while designing the city of Washington, D.C., did build the most famous Masonic symbol (the compass and the square) and the five-pointed pentagram into the city grid. . . . For over two hundred years those symbols have been hidden in plain sight."

(Note: The top point of the pentagram—formed by the intersections of Massachusetts Avenue, Rhode Island Avenue, Connecticut Avenue, Vermont Avenue, and K Street Northwest in the grid—lies at the White House. The hinge of the compass in the street grid lies at the Capitol with its vectors extending down Pennsylvania and Maryland avenues, while the accompanying square is formed by the intersection of Louisiana and Washington avenues.)

Though it is documented that both Washington and L'Enfant were Masons, it needs to be mentioned that Jefferson most probably wasn't, and indeed Jefferson was one of those involved with firing L'Enfant once the design (which did not include the Mall area that we know today) was under way.

Still, the Masonic influence is there and even played an integral part in the celebratory christening of the structures.

Meltzer further illuminates this matter, noting, "It is also true that on October 13, 1792, Maryland's Masonic Lodge Number 9 did lay the cornerstone of the White House in a Freemason ceremony. The same was true during the laying of the cornerstone of the U.S. Capitol Building, where George Washington himself presided over the Masonic ceremony. Washington's Masonic trowel was also used at the cornerstone laying of the Washington Monument, the U.S. Supreme Court, the Library of Congress, the National Cathedral and the Smithsonian."

Another frequent Masonic trope that is brought forward as evidence of the group's surreptitious influence on the government is the presence of a renowned Masonic sign on the seal of the United States (currently featured on the back of the standard dollar bill). The symbol in question is referred to as the All-Seeing Eye (allegedly belonging to the Great Architect, the omniscient deity acknowledged by all Masons), which is peeking out of the top of a Masonic-looking pyramid . . . but again it is noteworthy that the design of the currency and seal also features far more non-Masonic symbolism.

Indeed, if one is really trying to find such symbols, one might conclude that the embroidered inverted "V" in the fifth from the top white stripe of the Star-Spangled Banner that inspired Francis Scott Key's song (and is currently part of the Smithsonian collection) is also a Masonic symbol rather than something harmless like a family monogram (as historians believe).

This sort of makes the point that, yes, there is probably evidence of a Masonic influence that has been brought to bear by those founding fathers who were members . . . but in the long run probably nothing sinister was involved either.

These leaders were "social" men of a certain class in society who sought out the company of their contemporaries, for fun, profit, and, of course, professional advancement.

With the possible exception of Benjamin Franklin, whose eclectic tastes could be considered out of the mainstream (thus his membership in all the cited societies, including the more sordid ones), all of the others seem to have had memberships of convenience that provided them with camaraderie, commune, and a not inconsiderable amount of networking. As anyone with an interest in politics knows, those contacts are quite valuable if one is looking for financial support with one's candidacy for office.

Modern fictioneers aside, it is quite possible that the Masonic memberships of these men are more significant to the easily influenced readers two hundred years later than they were to the men themselves.

Lincoln's Dreams of Death

Though the curse of Tecumseh had already claimed its first victim, the possible occult nature of President William Henry Harrison's death had probably passed unnoticed. As a result, there was no reason to anticipate the oncoming death of another president so soon, nor was there any predilection to conceive of a death in office by anything other than natural causes.

Death was of course a possibility that everyone lived with but very few folks actually dwelled on. Abraham Lincoln, the sixteenth president, however, was far from just plain folks, and indeed death was a minor obsession for him.

Much has been written on the melancholia of the man and the miseries of his life, including the death of his first love, the loss of two of his sons, the trials of being married to the very unstable Mary Todd Lincoln, and, of course, the great weight of the office of the presidency itself. The growing pains of his United States had turned into a barbaric and bloody conflict that was threatening to tear the country asunder and scar it for all eternity. Part of this melancholia included a dream-inspired preoccupation with his own doppelgänger death.

One such vision occurred right before he took residence in the White House.

IT WAS JUST AFTER my election in 1860. . . . I was well tired out, and went home to rest, throwing myself down on a lounge in my chamber. Opposite where I lay was a bureau, with a swinging-glass upon it—[and here he got up and placed furniture to illustrate the position]—and, looking in that glass, I saw myself reflected, nearly at full length; but my face, I noticed, had two separate and distinct images, the tip of the nose of one being about three inches from the tip of the other. I was a little bothered, perhaps startled, and got up and looked in the glass, but the illusion vanished. On lying down again I saw it a second time—plainer, if possible, than before; and then I noticed that one of the faces was a little paler, say five shades, than the other. I got up and the thing melted away, and I went off and, in the excitement of the hour, forgot all about it—nearly, but not quite, for the thing would once in a while come up, and give me a little pang, as though something uncomfortable had happened. When I went home I told my wife about it, and a few days after I tried the experiment again, when [with a laugh], sure enough, the thing came again; but I never succeeded in bringing the ghost back after that, though I once tried very industriously to show it to my wife, who was worried about it somewhat. She thought it was "a sign" that I was to be elected to a second term of office, and that the paleness of one of the faces was an omen that I should not see life through the last term.

—as related by Noah Brooks in 1864
in *Harper's New Monthly Magazine*

Though the Brooks account might be considered morbidly ambiguous, there is no mistaking the subliminal intent of the dream the president reported experiencing just prior to that cursed night at Ford's Theater. According to Ward Hill Lamon, three days before the day of his assassination, Lincoln related the following account of a recent dream:

ABOUT TEN DAYS AGO, I retired very late. I had been up waiting for important dispatches from the front. I could not have been long in bed when I fell into a slumber, for I was weary. I soon began to dream. There seemed to be a death-like stillness about me. Then I heard subdued sobs, as if a number of people were weeping. I thought I left my bed and wandered downstairs. There the silence was broken by the same pitiful sobbing, but the mourners were invisible. I went from room to room; no living person was in sight, but the same mournful sounds of distress met me as I passed along. I saw light in all the rooms; every object was familiar to me; but where were all the people who were grieving as if their hearts would break? I was puzzled and alarmed. What could be the meaning of all this? Determined to find the cause of a state of things so mysterious and so shocking, I kept on until I arrived at the East Room, which I entered. There I met with a sickening surprise. Before me was a catafalque, on which rested a corpse wrapped in funeral vestments. Around it were stationed soldiers who were acting as guards; and there was a throng of people, gazing mournfully upon the corpse, whose face was covered, others weeping pitifully. "Who is dead in the White House?" I demanded of one of the soldiers. "The President," was his answer; "he was killed by an assassin." Then came a loud burst of grief from the crowd, which woke me from my dream. I slept no more that night; and although it was only a dream, I have been strangely annoyed by it ever since.

The aftermath of this conversation is as follows (from *Lincoln: An Account of His Personal Life, Especially of Its Springs of Action as Revealed and Deepened by the Ordeal of War* by Nathaniel Wright Stephenson):

HE TOLD THIS DREAM to Lamon and to Mrs. Lincoln. He added that after it had occurred, "the first time I opened the Bible, strange as it may appear, it was at the twenty-eighth chapter

of Genesis which relates the wonderful dream Jacob had. I turned
to other passages and seemed to encounter a dream or a vision
wherever I looked. I kept on turning the leaves of the Old Book, and
everywhere my eye fell upon passages recording matters strangely
in keeping with my own thoughts—supernatural visitations, dreams,
visions, etc."

But when Lamon seized upon this as text for his recurrent sermon
on precautions against assassination, Lincoln turned the matter into
a joke. The president claimed that he did not appear to interpret the
dream as foreshadowing his own death.

Lincoln called Lamon's alarm "downright foolishness."

Another dream on the last night of his life was a consolation. He
narrated it to Cabinet members when they met on April 14 (which
happened to be Good Friday). There was some anxiety with regard to
General William Tecumseh Sherman's movements in North Carolina.
Lincoln bade the Cabinet set their minds at rest. His dream of the
night before was one he had often had. It was a presage of great events.
In this dream he saw himself "in a singular and indescribable vessel,
but always the same . . . moving with great rapidity toward a dark and
indefinite shore." This dream had preceded all the great events of the
war. He believed it was a good omen.

The omens were indeed good for the Union.

The "downright foolishness" (Lincoln's words) of Lamon's alarm
was in reality all the president's as he ignored this occult warning of
the rapid approach of his own death by an assassin's bullet.

Chapter 9

The Presidents and Their Spiritual Advisers

In an 1863 pamphlet authored by "a Citizen of Ohio," the argument was made that Abraham Lincoln had fallen under the influence of spiritualists who had coerced him into instigating the War Between the States.

The introduction of the pamphlet, titled "Interior Causes of the War: The Nation Demonized, and Its President a Spirit-Rapper," states:

WE ARE INFORMED BY persons who profess to understand the secret condition of things at Washington, that Mr. Lincoln is not only a spiritualist of the abolitionist school, but has his media around him, and is, and has been, from the beginning of his term, directing the war under the direction of spirit rappings. Such men as Robert Dale Owen of Indiana, Judge Edmonds of New York, and Andrew Jackson Davis of New Jersey, are said to be constantly around him, advising him from the spirit world, and urging him onward in his abolition, death dealing policy. But it is not alone in these uncommissioned advisors that Mr. Lincoln finds spiritualistic support, nor are they their country's worst enemies, for they are honest enough to declare their reasons with their designs. But in the cabinet and in congress, and in various other official positions, are many many other men equally reliant on spiritual communications, and equally adherent to the rappings, but without the same honesty to declare their secret springs of action. Secretary Chase, Senator Wade, and Joshua R. Giddings, all of this state, are (if their spiritualistic friends may be relied upon) men of this particular stamp. Mr. Wade's wife is said to be one of the best mediums in Ohio, and through her he is said to be kept advised of interior objects. Messrs. Chase and Giddings may not be so fortunate in their families, but a little inquiry either at Cincinnati or Columbus, Ohio, will disclose the fact that both have for years been consulting the rappings.

Mr. Greely, of the *New York Tribune,* may also be included in the same list, although he voluntarily appeared in his paper, some years ago, and renounced all the faith, in the communications, which he once entertained. But this renunciation, we have understood, made only for a disguise, in order that he might operate more effectively on the public mind. Henry Ward Beecher has also through his paper, the "Independent" volunteered a denial, a denial not of his spiritual reliance, but of his being spiritually influenced in his preachings. Such a denial, of course, extends but a little way, and there leaves the apprehension that the greater point, the question of the reliance on the rappings, has been intentionally omitted. Mr. Beecher's whereabouts may be ambiguous; but it is a well known fact that, that the most ultra spiritualists of New York not only patronize his paper, but attend his meetings, and heartily approve of his discourses.

In these names may be seen a few, and but a few, of the men high in power and influence, who fancy themselves in possession of higher lights than those to which the country at large has ascended, and who, in consequence, assume a superiority, and from it as an assumed altitude, preach the doctrine of a "higher Law"—an authority above our civil polity.

The article called "McClellan's Dream" [see chapter 1, "The Visions of Washington"], which appeared in the spiritualistic papers, and also in extra sheets, about the time of that officer's appointment to the eastern army, may be trifling in itself, yet may some day lead to more disclosures. It may disclose a fellow feeling between the General and the president, in their reliance on the rappings, and on so display one, at least, of the causes which may have led to the General's appointment to the Potomac command. If a man believes my faith, I, of necessity, believe his. The General may have been rapped into command, but as the intelligence of familiar spirits is of all intelligence the most vacillating, it is highly probable that if the spirits rapped him into command at one sitting, they at another may have rapped him out again.

Mr. Lincoln is by no means neglectful of his spiritualistic friends, nor is he averse to having them around him, a fact which may not be not only be seen in his social relations, as above noticed, and in his particular attention to "Progressive Friends" (a new name for his kind of spiritualists), but it may be seen in some of his appointments; one of which, because of the relations which surround it, we will here notice. It is the appointment of a trance lecturer to a position at Washington within hailing distance of the president's mansion.

This lecturer for many years traveled over the northwestern country, and while at Springfield in Illinois, is said to have made Mr. Lincoln's house one of his points of stopping. But this latter we have heard of only since Mr. Lincoln's election, and as many things are said of men, after they acquire distinction, it may or may not be true. But this much we know to be reliable, that soon after Mr. Lincoln's inauguration, this same trance lecturer received an appointment to a position near the president, where he still is, ready at call to serve his Excellency, as the witch of Endor served the Hebrew king, to bring forth the spirits of the dead.

These facts may serve to awaken the American people to a sense of their condition—to point them to real causes, and to show them that they are subjects of a cruel and unparalleled imposition—

to unfold to them the reason why fifteen hundred million dollars of their property has already been worse than thrown away,—why three hundred thousand of their young men have been sent to untimely graves,—why the nation has been excessively vain,—why men have denounced negro slavery to deceive others until they deceived themselves,—why we destroyed a union, existing in mutual assent, and then in his name, as a deception, sought to establish another, founded on conquest and military power,—why the most formidable armies and navies, the world ever saw, have been rolled back by inferior numbers,—why we entered the contest with the world on our side, and now, near its conclusion, with all the world against us,—and lastly, though not least, why the sun of American greatness is rapidly sinking in a sea of fraternal blood.

Nature conforms to conditions. The miller is undisturbed by the rattles of his machinery; and the inhabitants of offensive localities become more unconscious of their odors. So too are the insane unconscious of their maladies. It is now so with the American people. They are mad, made so by an interior influence exerted on their minds.

Whether this article was merely an attempt by pro-southern detractors of the president to undermine both his credibility and the casus belli he relied on, or perhaps a smear piece by his northern detractors, who merely wanted to see him not reelected in hopes of a peacefully negotiated settlement to the war, or even interpreting it in its least cynical light, an impassioned antispiritualism piece first, and only secondarily an anti-Lincoln piece, there is no doubt that linking spiritualism and the presidency was not far from the chattering classes' minds.

The *Encyclopedia Britannica* defines spiritualism simply as "the belief, or practices based upon the belief, that departed souls hold intercourse with mortals, usually through a medium by means of physical phenomena or during abnormal mental states, such as trances."

In 1848, a trio of sisters with the family name Fox achieved a degree of notoriety as "spirit rappers," leading to widespread public interest and a promulgation of spiritualist beliefs and practices throughout the country. Many of these so-called mediums were proven to be charlatans out for a buck while others were sincere in their beliefs in their own powers and their desire to assist others through communications with the spirit plane.

The death of their son Willie Wallace Lincoln in 1862 from typhoid fever at the age of twelve may have been the pivotal event that drew the First Family into contact with spiritualists. Carl Sandburg's biography of Lincoln contains the following reference:

"[According to Orville Browning in reference to a carriage ride he took with First Lady Mary Todd Lincoln] Mrs. Lincoln told me she had been, the night before, with Old Isaac Newton, out to Georgetown, to see a Mrs. Laury, a spiritualist and she had made wonderful revelations to her about her little son Willy who died last winter, and also about things on the earth. Among other things she revealed that the cabinet were all enemies of the president, working for themselves, and that they would have to be dismissed."

This trip was obviously not an isolated case and there were numerous accounts around that the spiritualists were involved not just with the First Lady but with the president himself, and that they had even, as asserted by the pamphlet by "the citizen from Ohio," insinuated themselves into the president's inner circle.

Charles Shockle

The following account with the dateline of "Washington, April 23, 1863" was related by a reporter from the *Boston Gazette* by the name of Prior Melton, who first placed the story in *Herald of Progress* in May 1863 under the title "A Readable Sketch: Spiritualism at the White House." It was subsequently picked up by numerous other publications both pro- and antispiritualism and reprinted on numerous occasions, though apparently it never received a scrupulous vetting around the time of its publication in terms of its accuracy. Indeed the medium Charles Shockle does not appear in any other articles or records, and the private papers of various members of the president's party fail to mention this occasion either. One can even see a certain similarity to the newspaper accounts of the various Washington visions in some of the text. This is not to say that the record of this occurrence has been discredited, only that it has not been confirmed.

A FEW EVENINGS SINCE Abraham Lincoln, President of the United States, was induced to give a spiritual soiree in the crimson room at the White House, to test the wonderful alleged supernatural powers of Mr. Charles E. Shockle. It was my good fortune, as a friend of the medium, to be present, the party consisting of the President, Mrs. Lincoln, Mr. Welles, Mr. Stanton, and Mr. L—, of New York, and Mr. F—, of Philadelphia. We took our seats in the circle about 8 o'clock, but the President was called away shortly after the manifestations commenced, and the spirits, which had apparently assembled to convince him of the power, gave visible tokens of their displeasure at the President's absence, by pinching Mr. Stanton's ears and twitching Mr. Welles beard. He soon returned, but it was some time before harmony was restored, for the mishaps to the secretaries caused such bursts of laughter that the influence was very unpropitious. For some half hour the demonstrations were of a physical character—tables were moved and the picture of Henry Clay, which hangs on the wall, was swayed more than a foot, and two candelabras, presented by the Dey of Algiers to President Adams, were twice raised nearly to the ceiling.

It was nearly 9 o'clock before Shockle was fully under spiritual influence, and so powerful were the subsequent manifestations that twice during the evening restoratives were applied, for he was much weakened; and though I took no notes, I shall endeavor to give you as faithful an account as possible of what took place.

Loud rappings about 9 o'clock were heard directly beneath the President's feet, and Mr. Shockle stated that an Indian desired to communicate.

"Well, sir," said the President, "I should be happy to hear what his Indian majesty has to say. We have recently had a visitation from our red brethren, and it was the only delegation, black, white, or blue which did not volunteer some advice about the conduct of the war."

The medium then called for pencil and paper, and they were laid upon the table, in sight of all. A handkerchief was then taken from Mr. Stanton, and the materials were carefully concealed from sight. In less space of time than it has required me to write this, knocks were heard and the paper was uncovered. To the surprise of all present it read as follows:

"Haste makes waste, but delays cause vexations. Give vitality by energy. Use every means to subdue. Proclamations are useless; make a bold front and fight the enemy; leave traitors at home to the care of loyal men. Less note of preparation, less parade and policy-talk, more action. HENRY KNOX."

"That is not Indian talk, Mr. Shockle," said the President. "Who is Henry Knox?"

I suggested to the medium to ask who General Knox was, and before the words were from my lips the medium spoke in a strange voice: "the first Secretary of War."

"Oh, yes, General Knox," said the President who, turning to the Secretary, said: "Stanton that message is for you; it is from your predecessor."

Mr. Stanton made no reply.

"I should like to ask General Knox," said the President, "if it is within the scope of his ability to tell us when the rebellion will be put down."

In the same manner as before his message was received:

"Washington, Lafayette, Franklin, Wilberforce, Napoleon, and myself have held frequent consultations upon this point. There is something which our spiritual eyes cannot detect which appear well formed. Evil has come at times by removal of men from high positions, and there are those in retirement whose abilities should be made useful to hasten the end. Napoleon says concentrate your forces upon one point; Lafayette thinks that the rebellion will die of exhaustion; Franklin sees the end approaching, as the South must give up for want of mechanical ability to compete against Northern mechanics. Wilberforce sees hope only in a negro army." —"KNOX."

"Well," exclaimed the President, "opinions differ among the saints as well as among the sinners. They don't seem to understand running the machines among the celestials much better than we do. Their talk and advice sound very much like the talk of my cabinet—don't you think so, Mr. Welles?"

"Well, I don't know—I will think the matter over and see what conclusion to arrive at."

Heavy raps were heard and the alphabet was called for, when "That's what's the matter" was spelt out.

There was a shout of laughter, and Mr. Welles stroked his beard.

"That means, Mr. Welles," said the President, "that you are apt to be long-winded, and think the nearest way home is the longest way round. Short cuts in war times. I wish the spirits could tell us how to catch the *Alabama*."

The lights, which had been partially lowered, almost instantaneously became so dim that I could not see sufficiently to distinguish the features of any one in the room, and on the large mirror over the mantle-piece there appeared the most beautiful though supernatural picture ever beheld. It represented a sea view, the *Alabama* with all steam up flying from the pursuit of another large steamer. Two merchantmen in the distance were seen partially destroyed by fire. The picture changed, and the *Alabama* was seen at anchor under the shadow of an English fort—from which an English flag was waving. The *Alabama* was floating idly, not a soul on board, and no signs of life visible about her. The picture vanished, and in letters of purple appeared, "The English people demanded this of England's aristocracy."

"So England is to seize the *Alabama* finally?" said the President. "It may be possible; but Mr. Welles, don't let one gunboat or monitor less be built."

The spirits called for the alphabet, and again, "That's what's the matter," was spelt out.

"I see, I see," said the President. "Mother England thinks that what's sauce for the goose may be sauce for the gander. It may be tit, tat, too, hereafter. But it is not very complimentary to our navy, anyhow."

"We've done our best, Mr. President," said Mr. Welles. "I'm maturing a plan which, when perfected, I think, if it works well, will be a perfect trap for the *Alabama.*"

"Well, Mr. Shockle," remarked the President, "I have seen strange things and heard rather odd remarks, but nothing which convinces me, except the pictures, that there is anything very heavenly about all this. I should like, if possible, to hear what Judge Douglas says about this war."

"I'll try to get his spirit," said Mr. Shockle, "but it sometimes happens, as it did tonight in the case of the Indian, that though first impressed by one spirit, I yield to another more powerful. If perfect silence is maintained I will see if we cannot induce General Knox to send for Mr. Douglas."

Three raps were given, signifying assent to the proposition. Perfect silence was maintained, and after an interval of perhaps three minutes, Mr. Shockle rose quickly from his chair and stood up behind it, resting his left arm on the back, his right thrust into his bosom. In a voice such as no one could mistake who had ever heard Mr. Douglas, he spoke. I shall not pretend to quote the language. It was eloquent and choice. He urged the President to throw aside all advisers who hesitate about the policy to be pursued, and to listen to the wishes of the people, who would sustain him at all points if his aim was, as he believed it was, to restore the Union. He said their [sic] were Burrs and Blennerhassetts living, but that they would wither before the popular approval which would follow one or two victories, such as he thought must take place ere long. The turning point in this war will be the proper use of these victories— if wicked men in the first hours of success think it time to devote their attention to party, the war will be prolonged; but if victory is followed up by energetic action, all will be well.

"I believe that," said the President, "whether it comes from spirit or human."

Mr. Shockle was much prostrated after this, and at Mrs. Lincoln's request it was thought best to adjourn the dance, which, if resumed, I shall give you an account of.

Yours, as ever.

MELTON.

Nettie Colburn Maynard

Years after Lincoln's death, the subject of his involvement with the spiritualists is still a matter of debate. There is no doubt that his wife, Mary, engaged in such practices, but since *her* sanity even before his death is considered questionable, one can only wonder if the president and doting husband was just humoring his melancholic spouse.

When questioned on the general topic of séances at the White House, several of the former president's inner circle tried to quash such rumors, such as John G. Nicolay, who was Lincoln's private secretary during his presidency, and maintained in the *Daily Republican* of Decatur, Illinois, on October 24, 1891:

"Of course, I have no doubt that Mr. Lincoln, like a great many other men, might have had some curiosity as to spiritualism, and he might have attended some of these séances solely out of curiosity. But he was the last man in the world to yield to any other judgment than that arrived at by his own mature deliberation. He was not superstitious, nor did he have any spiritualistic tendencies. I have attended spiritualistic séances, not because I believed in them, but because I was curious to see the proceedings. They were such manifest humbugs that I usually came away disgusted. If President Lincoln ever attended séances, as alleged, it was with this same feeling of curiosity. But I do not remember that even curiosity ever impelled him to attend a séance. He had more important business on hand during those days. In any event I can say without the slightest qualification that a séance never occurred at the White House."

However, for every spinmeister in Lincoln's administration who wished to distance the memory of the great man from the "fad" that was considered by many to be the profession of charlatans preying on the weak-minded and gullible, there were an equal number of fairly high-profile figures in the field that attested to the president's affinity for this matter of the occult.

One of these prominent figures was a certain Nettie Colburn Maynard, the daughter of one of General George Brinton McClellan's staff officers who lent her "spiritual expertise" to the war effort, and to some accounts, to the president and his wife as well. In her 1917 memoir, *Was Abraham Lincoln a Spiritualist?: Or, Curious Revelations from the Life of a Trance Medium*, this medium is quite clear and specific about her relationship with both the president and his wife, and goes into great detail about some of their encounters as follows:

WHILE RIDING UP PENNSYLVANIA AVENUE
to Georgetown in a street car filled with a miscellaneous crowd
composed chiefly of officers and soldiers from the headquarters in
Georgetown, an incident came under my notice that I deem worthy
of record. It was a dull, rainy morning such as drives all pedestrians
indoors or under shelter, and the avenue above the Treasury building was practically deserted. Seated on the right-hand side of the
car, I faced the Treasury building.

As we turned the corner, and some distance ahead, I beheld the
tall figure of President Lincoln going with hurried strides toward the
White House. He wore an old-fashioned dress coat, the sleeves tight to
the arm and the right elbow torn so that his white shirt sleeve plainly
showed through, and he, seemingly unconscious of this discrepancy in
his dress, was pursuing his way with his head down as if in a profound
study. He wore a beaver hat that looked as well worn as his coat, and
in his right hand was a bundle of papers as though he had just come
from some office. As he neared the gate of the White House, a soldier
boy leaning on crutches, one leg drawn up, approached, and they nearly
collided, so absorbed was Mr. Lincoln in his thoughts.

Hastily looking up, seeing who was before him, he instantly removed his hat, the soldier boy doing the same. He then commenced
talking to him, and from his manner seemed to be inquiring as to
the cause of his lameness, while one hand went into his pocket.
As he drew it out, and was in the act of handing the soldier what
was in his hand, his back was to the street and he did not see the
loaded car which was then opposite. The soldier boys in the car,
however, saw him; one impulsively jerked the check-strap and the
car stopped; he shouted at the top of his lungs. "Three cheers for
Father Abraham" rent the air. They were given with a will.

He looked around, startled at the outburst so near him; acting
like a schoolboy caught in some dereliction of duty, thrust what he
had in the hand of the soldier, doffed his hat again, and with a smile

hurried out of sight into the grounds of the White House, followed by the cheers of soldiers, who witnessed in this kindness shown, unseen as he supposed, the man they loved in the President that ruled them.

I have seen President Lincoln under many aspects, and he never failed to evidence the man of kindly heart, tender feelings, and one replete with thoughtfulness for others, and one willing to serve the humblest where it did not conflict with his sense of duty.

... In the early fall of 1863 my friend and myself received a request from the Colonel Chrysler, at Saratoga, that we should go to Washington and see the President on behalf of him and his veterans, of whom he had raised three hundred. About this time there was strong call for reinforcements, and as fast as troops were enlisted they were forwarded to Washington and sent "to the Camp of Distribution," so called, and scattered through the different army corps to fill up depleted companies. Colonel Chrysler's fear was that this fate would await his command; and his ambition was to raise his brigade and so obtain the command thereof. He had confidence in my power to reach the President, and he had also confidence in the unseen powers that controlled me, and he earnestly requested that I should make the effort in his behalf, offering to defray all expenses, which he did.

We went at once, going directly to our friend Mrs. Cosby, on Capitol Hill, who received us with joy and surprise, as she had not expected us until later. I told her the purpose of our coming and requested her to accompany me to see Mr. Lincoln. As we could not go at once, we decided upon making the venture the following day. Morning came and brought with it an important visitor, who called on our friend. This person was Mr. Joshua Speed. We were introduced to him; and Anna, in her gentle but forcible way, informed him of my peculiar gift, and that of my friend. While we were talking Parnie was controlled by what proved to be the spirit of an old

coloured man—a former slave who was in the family of Mr. Speed,
and who identified himself with his old master by expressing his
thanks that he was granted his request "to be buried under the tree
where in his old age he used to sit, and where (if memory serves
correctly) he had died."

Mr. Speed acknowledged that this was very strange and singular,
and afterward questioned us both clearly and closely in regard to
our peculiar gifts. The forenoon passed quickly; and as Mr. Speed
was about to leave us, Mrs. Cosby told him of our desire to visit the
President. She asked him for a letter of introduction. Smiling, he said,
"Surely, you need no letter of introduction to him."

She answered, "It has been some time since I have seen him,
and I would be pleased to have a letter from you."

He sat down at her desk, and quickly indited (sic) a genial note
of introduction, including my name also in the letter. I will here state
that a few months previously Mr. Cosby had been superseded in
his consulship, owing to the fact that he had been reported to our
government "as giving entertainments to the representatives of the
Southern Confederacy, at the port where he was stationed." I think
it was this fact that led Mrs. Cosby to desire a letter of introduction to Mr. Lincoln, fearing that he might believe that she also held
disloyal sentiments. The day was too far spent when Mr. Speed took
his departure for us to think of visiting the White House.

At ten o'clock next morning we stood at the portals of the
White House, where the genial Edward received our cards and letter, and were led soon after into the presence of Mr. Lincoln.

Mr. Lincoln was alone. He greeted Mrs. Cosby with a most serious but kindly deference in his manner, and he gave me his usual
kindly greeting of, "How do you do, Miss Nettie?—glad to see you
back among us." There was an awkward silence for a moment. He
asked us to be seated. Then, turning to Mrs. Cosby, he remarked,
"We have not met, Mrs. Cosby, since it was my un-pleasant duty to

banish your husband from the country." She replied, "No, Mr. Lincoln; and I trust, when the full truth is known, Mr. Cosby will prove less culpable than the report caused him to appear." A slight pause, and then he remarked: "In public life we are compelled to forego all claims save those of duty, and in a critical time like the present, when the nation's life is in our hands, we must often seem to our friends unduly stern and relentless." "Say no more," remarked Mrs. Cosby in her gentle way; "I fully recognize your position, Mr. Lincoln, and am too loyal a woman to the interests of the Union to question anything which you may deem proper to do."

I shall not forget the grace and dignity of manner that governed my friend as she uttered these words, which indelibly impressed themselves upon my memory, and seemed equally to impress Mr. Lincoln, for he remarked, "I thank you for your loyalty," and "I fear that the same does not exist with all our lady residents in Washington."

During this time, he had held Mr. Speed's letter in his hand, and now turning to it said, "I see you are acquainted with my friend Speed." "Yes," she replied; "he gave me a pleasant call yesterday." "He is a good fellow," remarked Mr. Lincoln; and, after some few words concerning their early associations, looked up with his genial smile, and said, "I was with him the night he settled it about his marriage with the widow. I was walking along the road when he overtook me with his wagon and asked me to get in. We rode together until we reached her house, and there stopped for the night. I could see that Josh had something on his mind, but I did not know what that something was until I was left to go to bed alone. Towards morning Joshua came to bed, and, awakening me, informed me of the important fact that it was settled between him and the widow."

I now see the President as he then looked, seated in a big armchair, one leg thrown over the arm, his hands clasped behind his head, talking to us in this pleasant, familiar strain; and, as Mrs. Cosby afterwards said, "We felt that he was, under the circumstances, endeavoring to cover the embarrassment of our meeting, bearing in mind the removal of Mr. Cosby from office." As he concluded, Mrs. Cosby turned to me, and said, "Miss Nettie is a petitioner to-day." He looked at me in all kindness and asked how he could serve me. In as few words as possible I related the dilemma of my acquaintance, and his request that I should lay the matter before the President, feeling that if he fully understood the determination and purpose he would not permit the troops to be scattered.

"By the way," he remarked, "I think I have received a telegram from your friend," and stepping to his table in the centre of the room he picked up a dispatch and read aloud: "We are coming, Father Abraham, three hundred veterans strong—M. H. Chrysler, commanding."

The President quietly chuckled as he read it, and, turning to me, said: "I really have no power in the matter; but think I can somewhat influence the decision of the commanding officers. To tell the truth, it is unwise for me to interfere in any of the regulations connected with the army. You have no idea what a time I had when this war first broke out. When I issued my call for the first 75,000 men I was as ignorant as a child regarding the best course to pursue. Regiments were poured into Washington, and were lying about without shelter and without sufficient provisions. The troops were clamoring at the doors here for orders, and I was harassed and perplexed, not knowing what to do. At last Gov. Morgan, of New York, wrote me that it was impossible for him to fill the quota of his State until I called my recruiting officers from the field. I thought his letter impertinent, and took no notice of it. He, with others, then visited me, and explained the situation. Two recruiting parties were in the field—one in my name, contesting for the enlisting soldier; and one under the officers of the State, trying to obtain regiments to fill the demand—I, meanwhile, having made peremptory demand on the Governors of the States to forward their proportion.

"My mistake was apparent, for I had *granted the right to raise troops to every man who had applied,* and, therefore, had unwittingly checked or balked my own purpose. Of course I then cancelled all orders, and left the affairs where they should be—*in the hands of the Governors of the respecting States.* As a result, order was soon restored. So, you see, my young friend, the difficulty in this case. But I will tell you what I will do. I will give you a line to the Secretary of War, and request him to send these men to the Camp of Instruction until the brigade is completed— if he finds it possible to do so." He wrote a line to this effect, signing and handing it to me, and, after a few more words of kindness and explanation, shook us cordially by the hand and bade us good day.

Here, again, was the kindly and genial spirit of President Lincoln clearly shown, in that he should take the pains to explain to me his inability to comply with my request, confessing at the same time his deficiency in knowledge when war first made its demands upon him; going into an account of matters he need not have named, when without a word he might have dismissed us, as most likely any other official in Washington would have done. But it was ever the characteristic of this man, so great in goodness, that he avoided wounding the feelings of the humblest, and ever sought to work in perfect harmony with all of his people.

Being too late to see the Secretary of War that afternoon, we returned home. The next morning my friend was ill with a sick-headache, and Parnie and I went to the War Department and asked to see Secretary Stanton.

We held the paper Mr. Lincoln had given us, on which was written, "The Secretary will receive Miss Colburn and hear her statement. —A. LINCOLN."

This paper procured us instant admission to the presence of the Secretary, who received us with a very stern, unbending countenance, that boded ill for the request. In trembling tones I stated the case, and remarked that the rigid orders surrounding my soldier friends prevented their getting leave of absence to prefer this request in person. Glancing at the paper which he held in his hand containing Mr. Lincoln's name, he said, "Why did you come to me? Mr. Lincoln has full power in this matter. Why didn't he attend to it?" As was often the case in an emergency, I felt the hand of an unseen guide on my shoulder, warning me to be careful of my reply; and I heard the words issue from my lips without any volition of my own: "I supposed, as Secretary of War, you were the proper person to apply to in this case. I knew how hard it was to get to your presence, and I asked Mr. Lincoln for this paper." His countenance changed instantly, and in the kindest tones imaginable bade us be seated, took down the name of Col. Chrysler, the number of men under his command, and all the circumstances attending the subject, saying kindly, "I will see that this is attended to at once," and politely showed us out.

Some time afterwards, in relating this circumstance to a friend in Washington, I was informed that the good Secretary was a little jealous of his prerogatives, and looked with unfriendly eyes upon any interference from the White House. Be this as it may, I know that my politic answer to his irate question, *for which I was not responsible,* seemed to change the face of matters and favorably shape results for our friends of the camp, who, when visiting us a few days later, informed us in high glee that they were ordered to remain at the Camp of Instruction until their brigade was fully completed, and also given full power to enlist veterans for that purpose.

EARLY IN 1864 WE were the guests of Mr. and Mrs. Somes. Mrs. Somes seldom went into society, owing to the loss of her eldest son and her preference for home life. She was a lady of remarkable ability, refined and gentle manners, a devoted wife and mother, and a sincere Christian. My friend, Miss Hannum, and I soon called at the White House, to pay our respects to the President and his wife, and were received with the greatest cordiality.

We remained but a short time, but were both particularly struck by Mr. Lincoln's careworn appearance. His old genial smile was the same, as he expressed the hope that we had come to spend the winter. A few days later Mrs. Somes received a note cordially inviting herself and husband to spend an evening at the White House, and requesting her to bring the young ladies, meaning Miss Hannum and myself. At first Mrs. Somes was inclined to refuse, but yielding to her husband's solicitation, and our wishes, she consented. In her note Mrs. Lincoln said she desired her to meet a friend, and wished to see if she (Miss Pinkie) would be able to tell who it was. We reached the Executive Mansion at half-past eight, and were ushered into the Red Parlour, where the madam received us with great kindness, and presented us in turn to a distinguished, soldierly-looking gentleman, who was wrapped in a long military cloak, completely concealing his person and every evidence of rank. She did not call him by name, apologizing for not doing so, and saying she desired first to see if our friends could tell who he was, adding that she would duly present him afterwards. I saw that Mr. Somes recognized him instantly, but he gave no hint of his identity. My friend and myself re-moved our wraps, but Mrs. Somes declined, simply loosening hers. A pleasant half hour followed, when Mr. Lincoln joined us. After a cordial greeting all around, he wearily seated himself in an arm-chair and remarked, "I am very busy and must forego the pleasure of conversation and ask our little friend here to see what can be given us to-night as briefly as may be, for my Cabinet is awaiting my return."

Silence fell upon the group, and I was shortly entranced. What here follows was related to me on our return home by Mr. and Mrs. Somes and my friend. A strong, powerful presence seemed to have possession of me, directing first its entire attention to Mr. Lincoln. The substance of the remarks related to the condition of the Freedmen in and around Washington, declaring their condition deplorable in the extreme, that they were herding together like cattle in the open air, with little or no shelter, half fed and half clothed, while the manner of their existence was a reproach to the country, throwing down, as it did, all safeguards to morality and decency. A terrible picture was presented concerning the thousands thus rendered homeless and dependent upon the government, through the exigencies of war and the proclamation of Freedom.

While the spirits realized fully the many heavy cares resting upon the President, there was a duty to perform that could not be neglected—a duty that demanded immediate attention. They counseled him in the strongest terms to prove the truth of their statements, extravagant as they seemed, by appointing a special committee, whose duty it should be to investigate the condition of these people, and to receive their report in person, and on no account to receive it at second hand. They further advised that for this committee he should select men who were not burdened with other cares, that their minds might be given entirely to their work, for, if they did their duty well, he would see the necessity at once of organizing a separate bureau to control and regulate all the affairs connected with the Freedmen.

While I cannot, at this late day, give a more minute account of the instructions thus given, I have presented the main points. The powers controlling me then directed their attention to the gentleman in the military cloak. They at once addressed him as "General," saying that his cloak did not disguise from their eyes the evidence of the noble sacrifice he had laid on his country's altar, nor the glittering stars he so merited, for he had royally won them by his patriotic devotion to his country. They extended my hand to him, which he accepted, rising and bowing with the same courtesy and dignity that characterized him towards all; and whatever may have been his private opinions concerning mediumship and Spiritualism, his manner was that of a courteous and true gentleman. A few words of greeting were then spoken to all—a final word of encouragement and strength spoken to the President—when the influence changed, and "Pinkie," the little Indian maiden, took possession of my organism, and after greeting the President and Mrs. Lincoln in her usual manner, turned at once to the stranger, addressing him as "Crooked Knife," her Indian name for him, thus giving to Mrs. Lincoln the test she required, as it was thus ascertained that "Pinkie" recognized him as the General of whom she had often spoken in former circles when relating events that were taking place on distant battlefields.

While she was talking in her childish way, Mr. Lincoln excused himself, returning to his Cabinet meeting. When I awoke a half hour later, I found myself standing in front of the gentleman whom I had met that evening for the first time, and saw that his clear, piercing eyes were fixed wholly upon me. Mrs. Lincoln now hastened to cover my embarrassment by duly presenting us to all. This officer was Major-General Sickels (now Sheriff of New York City), who laid aside his cloak, revealing his whole uniform and a crutch which, until that moment had been concealed. This was the first and only time my friend and myself ever met this famous general, although, as I have stated, he and other generals were often mentioned in communications that were made by me to the President and his wife, while giving them tidings of the true state of affairs at the front, which communications were afterwards fully confirmed when reliable particulars were received. Of this I was assured on more than one occasion by Mrs. Lincoln.

It was after eleven o'clock when our carriage was announced, and as we departed the General stood by the side of Mrs. Lincoln, shaking hands with us in turn as we passed from their presence. I vividly recall the scene; the bright fire in the open grate, sending a genial warmth through the room; a large pyramid of flowers and palms in the centre of the apartment, giving a look of richness to the scene; while a marble bust of Mr. Lincoln, just received, and to which Mrs. Lincoln had called our attention earlier in the evening, stood in front of the large pier-glass, seeming almost lifelike in the shifting shadows made by the gas-light and waving palms. The scene was one never to be forgotten.

DURING THE LATTER PART of February, and the month of March, I had a number of séances with President Lincoln and his wife; but, as there were no other witnesses, and as they did not inform me of the nature of the communications, I cannot speak as to their nature, but simply allude to the fact. These séances took place by appointment. At the close of one, Mrs. Lincoln would make an appointment, engaging me to come at a certain hour of the day, which usually would be in the vicinity of one o'clock, the time when Mr. Lincoln usually partook of his luncheon, which generally occupied about half to three-quarters of an hour. There was another meeting with Mr. Lincoln which is interesting and of considerable value. Shortly after my return to Washington, and while visiting Major Chorpenning one evening, Mr. Somes called. After an exchange of compliments, he stated that he had been requested to have me attend a séance, and as the same was of a private character he was not at liberty to say more. We all suspected the truth, however, and I instantly made ready to accompany him.

AFTER ENTERING THE CARRIAGE provided for the occasion, he informed us that our destination was the White House, explaining that while at the War Department that afternoon he had met Mr. Lincoln coming from Secretary Stanton's office. Mr. Somes bowed to the President and was passing onward when Mr. Lincoln stopped him, asking whether Miss Colburn was still in the city, and if so, whether it were possible to have her visit the White House that evening. Upon a reply in the affirmative to both questions, Mr. Lincoln remarked, "Please bring her to the White House at eight or nine o'clock, but consider the matter confidential."

BY THE TIME MR. SOMES had completed his recital we were at the door of that historic mansion, and a servant who was evidently on the watch for us, quickly opened the door and we were hurried upstairs to the executive chamber, where Mr. Lincoln and two gentlemen were awaiting our coming. Mr. Lincoln gave an order to the servant, who retired, and a moment later Mrs. Lincoln entered. I am satisfied from what followed that she was summoned on my account to place me more at ease than otherwise, under the circumstances, would have been the case. Mr. Lincoln then quietly stated that he wished me to give them an opportunity to witness something of my "rare gift," as he called it, adding, "you need not be afraid, as these friends have seen something of this before."

THE TWO GENTLEMEN REFERRED to were evi-
dently military officers, as was indicated by the stripe upon their
pantaloons, although their frock coats, buttoned to the chin, effectu-
ally concealed any insignia or mark of rank. One of these gentlemen
was quite tall and heavily built, with auburn hair and dark eyes, and
side whiskers, and of decided military bearing. The other gentleman was of average height, and I somehow received the impression
that he was lower in rank than his companion. He had light brown
hair and blue eyes, was quick in manner, but deferential towards his
friend, whose confirmation he involuntarily sought or indicated by
his look of half appeal while the conversation went on.

WE SAT QUIET FOR a few moments before I became
entranced. One hour later I became conscious of my surroundings,
and was standing by a long table, upon which was a large map of the
Southern States. In my hand was a lead pencil, and the tall man, with
Mr. Lincoln, was standing beside me, bending over the map, while the
younger man was standing on the other side of the table, looking curi-
ously and intently at me. Somewhat embarrassed, I glanced around to
note Mrs. Lincoln quietly conversing in another part of the room. The
only remarks I heard were these: "It is astonishing," said Mr. Lincoln,
"how every line she has drawn conforms to the plan agreed upon."
"Yes" answered the older soldier, "it is very astonishing." Looking up,
they both saw that I was awake, and they instantly stepped back, while
Mr. Lincoln took the pencil from my hand and placed a chair for me.

Then madam and Mr. Somes at once joined us, Mr. Somes asking, "Well, was everything satisfactory?" "Perfectly," responded Mr.
Lincoln; "Miss Nettie does not seem to require eyes to do anything," smiling pleasantly. The conversation then turned, designedly, I
felt, to commonplace matters.

Shortly afterwards, when about leaving, Mr. Lincoln said to us in a low voice, "It is best not to mention this meeting at present." Assuring him of silence upon the question, we were soon again on our way to the majors.

Mr. Somes informed me that he heard enough in the opening remarks of the spirit to convince him that the power controlling knew why I had been summoned. He said I walked to the table unaided and requested that a pencil be handed me, after which the President requested Mr. Somes and Mrs. Lincoln to remain where they were at the end of the room. "In accordance with this request," said Mr. Somes, "we paid no attention to what was being said or done, further than to notice you tracing lines upon the map, and once one of the gentlemen re-sharpened the pencil for you." I never knew the purport of this meeting, nor can I say that Mr. Somes ever heard more regarding the strange affair. That it was important may be supposed, for those were not days for the indulgence of idle curiosity in any direction, nor was Mr. Lincoln a man to waste his time in giving exhibitions in occult science for the amusement of his friends. . . .

The impressions left upon my mind could not be otherwise than gratifying, in finding myself the recipient of such unusual attentions, and, for the occasion, the central figure in what appeared to be a mysterious and momentous consultation. Had it been simply an experiment to test my mediumship, Mr. Somes and Mrs. Lincoln would have been included in the group that gathered around the table. I am confident that my services were appreciated, and that the spiritual guidance which found utterance through my lips was confirmatory of the plans which they had already prepared. As in this instance, so in many others, has this powerful aid been called upon and used to advantage, to further important national and personal interests, and accomplish results that simple human knowledge could not achieve. Mr. Lincoln's fancy for poetry and song inclined towards those melodies which appealed to his emotional nature, as is illustrated by his keen appreciation of Mrs. Laurie's *Bonnie Doon,* and his favorite poem, *Why Should the Spirit of Mortal Be Proud?* I remember hearing him refer to the touching poem upon an occasion of peculiar interest, at which time he recited a part of it applying the verses to the occasion in a very pleasant and happy manner. This incident is worthy of appearing in print:

One morning in January, 1863, Mrs. Laurie desired me to go to the White House and inquire after Mrs. Lincoln's health. Mrs. Laurie had visited Mrs. Lincoln the previous day, and found her prostrated by one of her severe head-aches. It was about eleven o'clock when I called. Upon sending up my name and inquiry to Mrs. Lincoln, I was requested to walk upstairs to her rooms, where I found Mr. and Mrs. Lincoln, a gentleman, and two ladies. I was cordially received by Mr. and Mrs. Lincoln, and presented to the guests, whose names were not mentioned, and when I noticed their glances, I knew that they had been told I was a medium. After explaining my errand and being about to withdraw, Mrs. Lincoln asked whether I felt equal to the task of a séance. Noticing that all were expectant, I signified my willingness and reseated myself.

After Mrs. Lincoln had assisted me to remove my wraps, she requested that the friends present do the same. They declined. Whereupon the gentleman, who was their escort, laughingly remarked, as he indicated the lady nearest him: "It is useless to urge Anna, Mrs. Lincoln, for she thinks she looks better in her new bonnet." To which Anna replied, "That she believed she did, and felt very proud of it." Mr. Lincoln, who was seated, raised his hands with a comical gesture, and quoted a part of his favorite poem, *Why Should the Spirit of Mortal Be Proud?* The gentleman said, "You are familiar with that poem?" To which the president replied, "Perfectly; it is a favorite of mine; and, let me ask, what could be finer in expression than the lines:—'The maid on whose cheek, on whose brow, in whose eye, Shone beauty and pleasure,—her triumphs are by; And the memory of those who loved and praised, Are alike from the minds of the living erased.'" Continuing to the line:—"'Have quietly mingled their bones in the dust.'"

At this point I became unconscious, and awoke a half hour later to find the company betraying much emotion, and while recovering myself, they talked together in low tones, and in an animated manner. This was interrupted by Mr. Lincoln rousing himself with an effort, saying: "I must go, and am afraid I have already stayed too long." Shaking hands with his visitors, he turned in his kind way to me, and, while warmly shaking my hand, said: "I thank you, Miss Nettie, for obliging us; we have deeply enjoyed our little circle."

As he left the room, the others expressed the same sentiment; and as I was preparing to don my bonnet and shawl, Mrs. Lincoln requested me to wait. She rang the bell for the servant, who soon after returned with two beautiful bouquets, one of which she said was for Mrs. Laurie, the other for myself. The party then shook hands with me, rising as they did so. I was treated by them with the same courtesy as would have been offered any friend or old acquaintance.

[IN 1864] A FEW weeks later found us again in Washington City, in response to urgent solicitations on the part of friends, and we were the guests of Major Chorpenning and his wife. Major George Chorpenning was the first man to carry the United States mail across the Rocky Mountains, from Salt Lake City to San Francisco, under a contract with our government, which he had entered into many years previous to the time of which I am speaking, and which was annulled through the false representations of enemies, who coveted, and finally obtained, his position. When I

first met him, he was engaged in vigorously prosecuting his claim
against the government for damages sustained by the annulment of
his contract. He was generous and hospitable to a fault, while his
wife, a brilliant society lady, entertained in a manner that insured
the acceptance of their invitations. A brilliant company assembled in
their parlors once a week, and the evenings were always very en-
joyable. Nearly every reception, by unanimous request, was turned
into a spiritual circle, and I here met many gentlemen from both
branches of Congress.

These pleasant social gatherings are among the most pleasant
memories of my Washington experiences. Tuesday afternoons we
usually attended Mrs. Lincoln's receptions, often meeting there
the ladies and gentlemen who graced our own. It was during this
memorable winter of '64 and '65, when the Rebellion was in its
death throes, that I knew of the visits of Charles Colchester and
Charles Foster [two well-known mediums of that time] to the
White House, and of their sittings with President Lincoln. Through
them and through myself, he received warnings of his approaching
fate; but his fearless, confident nature disregarded the warnings
he received.

It was during the last days of February, when the city was being
filled to its utmost capacity by people from all parts of the country,
to witness the second inauguration of President Lincoln, that I received a dispatch from my home telling me my father was dangerously ill, and to come to him at once. Having an appointment at the
White House for the following week, I hastened with my friend,
Miss Hannum, to the Executive Mansion to inform Mrs. Lincoln of
the necessity that called me away. She was out, and we proceeded
upstairs to the ante-room, adjacent to Mr. Lincoln's office, hoping
for a last word with him.

It was two o'clock in the afternoon, and during the last days
of the expiring Congress, and the waiting-room was filled with

members from both Houses, all anxious to get a word with the President. Mr. Ingersoll and a number of others I knew were there, and it seemed doubtful of our obtaining an interview. Mr. Ingersoll smilingly asked if I expected to have an interview with Mr. Lincoln. I replied, "I hope so, as I am about to leave the city." He remarked, he feared it was doubtful, as he and many others had been waiting many hours for a chance to speak with him and had failed.

Edward, the faithful and devoted usher of the White House, was passing to and fro taking in cards to Mr. Lincoln's office. Calling him to me, I explained that I wished to see the President for one brief moment, to explain why I could not keep my engagement the following week; and giving him my card, bade him watch for an opportunity when Mr. Lincoln would be parting from those that were with him, and then placed my card in his hand, telling him I would detain him but an instant.

Half an hour went by, when Edward approached and bade us follow him. Mr. Ingersoll, with whom we had been talking, bade us laughingly to speak a good word for him, and we were soon ushered into Mr. Lincoln's presence. He stood at his table, busily looking over some papers, but laid them down and greeted us with his usual genial smile. In as few words as possible, knowing how precious was his time, we informed him of the cause of our unseasonable call, stating I had been summoned home by a telegram telling me my father was dangerously ill. Looking at me with a quizzical smile, he said, "But cannot our friends from the upper country tell you whether his illness is likely to prove fatal or not?" I replied that I had already consulted with our friends, and they had assured me that his treatment was wrong, and that my presence was needed to effect a cure. Turning to my friend, he said laughingly, "I didn't catch her, did I?"

Then turning to me, he said, "I am sorry you cannot remain to witness the inauguration, as no doubt you wish." "Indeed, we would enjoy it," I replied, "but the crowd will be so great we will not be able to see you, Mr. Lincoln, even if we remain." "You could not help it," he answered, drawing his tall figure to its full height, and glancing at my friend in an amused way, "I shall be the tallest man there." "That is true," my friend responded, "in every sense of the word." He nodded pleasantly at the compliment, and then turning to me remarked, "But what do our friends say of us now?" "What they predicted for you, Mr. Lincoln, has come to pass," I answered, "and you are to be inaugurated the second time." He nodded his head and I continued, "But they also re-affirm that the shadow they have spoken of still hangs over you. He turned half impatiently away and said, "Yes, I know. I have letters from all over the country from your kind of people—mediums, I mean—warning me against some dreadful plot against my life. But I don't think the knife is made, or the bullet run, that will reach it. Besides, nobody wants to harm me." A feeling of sadness that I could not conceal nor account for came over me and I said, "Therein lies your danger, Mr. President—your over-confidence in your fellow men."

The old melancholy look that had of late seemed lifted from his face now fell over it, and he said in his subdued, quiet way, "Well, Miss Nettie, I shall live till my work is done, and no earthly power can prevent it. And then it doesn't matter so that I am ready—and that I ever mean to be." Brightening again, he extended a hand to each of us, saying, "Well, I suppose I must bid you good-bye, but we shall hope to see you back again next fall."

"We shall certainly come," we replied, *"if you are here,"* without thinking of the doubts our words implied. "It looks like it now," he answered, and walking with us to a side door, with another cordial shake of the hand, we passed out of his presence for the last time. Never again would we meet his welcome smile.

. . . It should be borne in mind that all my meetings with Mr. Lincoln were at periods of special import, and upon occasions when he was in need of aid and direction. After the "circle," which he attended, he invariably left with a brighter and happier look, evidencing the benefit in part which he experienced from that which had been imparted to him.

It is also noteworthy that various accounts of the work of another noted spiritualist of the time, Cora Richmond, turned her attentions elsewhere after Lincoln's death and started to consult with those U.S. senators who were apparently working in opposition to his successor, Andrew Johnson. Richmond was undoubtedly known to both the president and his wife, as she was definitely part of the Washington spiritualist circle.

In 1883 she returned to Washington, D.C., and delivered an address titled "A Message to the Nation," where it is alleged that she channeled the spirit of the late President Garfield.

But putting this all into perspective, it is also claimed by her followers that she consulted with President U. S. Grant, who had denied *any* affiliation with spiritualism. In fact the *Trenton (N.J.) Times*, December 6, 1883, emphatically stated on his behalf: "General Grant denies that he is a Spiritualist. Of course he is not a Spiritualist. He is a tobacconist."

'Nuff said.

The President
and the Vampire

Andrew Johnson, the seventeenth president, is best known for a variety of less-than-stellar reasons.

He succeeded Abraham Lincoln after the sixteenth president's assassination.

He was the first president impeached by Congress. (Actually, Congress attempted to impeach him twice, though only one went to trial, and even that one failed to result in a conviction.)

He presided over the beginnings of the period known as post–Civil War Reconstruction, and he failed to be reelected to the presidency.

Among his presidential papers is the following missive:

To all to whom these Presents shall come,
GREETING:

Whereas, at the October term 1866, of the United States Circuit Court for the District of Massachusetts, one James Brown was convicted of murder and sentenced to be hung.

And whereas, I am assured by the United States District Attorney, Marshal and others, that there were certain mitigating circumstances in this case which render him a proper object of executive clemency;

Now, therefore, be it known, that I, Andrew Johnson, President of the United States of America, in consideration of the premises, divers other good and sufficient reasons me thereunto moving, do herby commute the said sentence of death imposed upon the said James Brown to imprisonment at hard labor in the Massachusetts State Prison at Charlestown, Massachusetts, for the term of his natural life.

Thus in January 1867, Johnson exercised one of his executive powers and commuted the death sentence of a convicted murderer—which on its face value alone was not really an act noteworthy of history. The presidential power to pardon is granted under Article II, Section 2 of the Constitution ("The President . . . shall have power to grant reprieves and pardons for offenses against the United States, except in cases of impeachment") giving the chief executive the power to pardon, commute, and/or grant clemency as he alone sees fit.

Indeed, Johnson was well on his way to setting an, up to that point in the history of the United States, new record for the number of pardons and commutations he was to issue during his tenure. By the end of his besieged presidency, Lincoln's successor had issued over 650 pardons, more than any previous president. This list included such notables as Edmund Spangler and Samuel Arnold, who were part of the plot to kill his predecessor, as well as Dr. Samuel Mudd, who was later tied to that conspiracy by merely providing medical assistance to a man with a broken leg who, unbeknownst to the good doctor at the time, turned out to be presidential assassin John Wilkes Booth. Johnson also issued a rather sweeping pardon of all Confederate soldiers who by their very action of serving in the Confederate military could have been held and convicted of treason and/or sedition through his Christmas Day 1868 amnesty. Johnson also signed an executive order that extended to all federal prisoners a New York state clemency program that provided so-called time off for good behavior.

Obviously, the seventeenth president was just a forgiving sort of guy (perhaps due to his own survival of both an assassination plot and an impeachment action by Congress), so the commutation of the sentence of a minor murderer seems hardly noteworthy . . . well, at least at the time.

Now skip ahead twenty-five years.

On November 4, 1892, the following article ran in the *Brooklyn Eagle* newspaper in the fourth column on page one:

A HUMAN VAMPIRE AND A MURDERER
The Terrible Record of a Maniac Convict—
Removed to an Asylum

COLUMBUS, O., NOVEMBER 4—Deputy United States Marshal Williams of Cincinnati has removed James Brown, a deranged United States prisoner, from the Ohio penitentiary to the national asylum at Washington, D.C. The prisoner fought like a tiger against being removed.

Twenty-five years ago he was charged with being a vampire and living on human blood. He was a Portuguese sailor and shipped on a fishing smack from Boston up the coast in 1867. During the trip two of the crew were missing and an investigation made. Brown was found one day in the hold of the ship sucking the blood from the body of one of the sailors. The other body was found at the same place and had been served in a similar manner. Brown was returned to Boston and convicted of murder and sentenced to be hanged. President Johnson commuted the sentence to imprisonment for life.

After serving fifteen years in Massachusetts he was transferred to Ohio prison. He has committed two murders since his confinement. When being taken from the prison he believed that he was on his way to execution and resisted accordingly.

The occasion for the media to revisit this case was obviously the prisoner's transfer to the mental institution, but more noteworthy is the first question that obviously comes to pass—why did the *Brooklyn Eagle* label Brown a vampire? Was this done through extensive investigative reporting (which isn't likely given the meager means of the

Brooklyn Eagle at the time and the lack of prominence the story was given, even though it was on the front page), or was it an attempt to sensationalize a routine story with Grand Guignol details that might thrill gullible readers? (Bram Stoker's sensational novel *Dracula* was still five years away from publication and mainstream success, thus leaving the concept of vampires more to the realm of folklore and superstition for the average *Brooklyn Eagle* reader, who was probably unacquainted with Stoker's literary precursors Sheridan Le Fanu, John Polidori, and William Beckford.)

Evidently the second- and third-hand "evidence" they used more directly relates to some sailor's stories of Brown's exploits prior to the murders in question for which he was actually convicted.

As it was related to the press after the fact, James Brown was actually Jem Brown of Liverpool, who had supposedly died in an 1866 cholera epidemic. His body was disposed of along with the other unfortunate victims of the outbreak in a mass grave—at least that's what was on the public record until he was later seen prowling the shadows of the back alleys near a tavern known as the Duck House pub, frequented by sailors.

Soon thereafter it is alleged that he signed on to a ship bound for America mere days before a prostitute came forward with a shocking story. This woman of ill repute claimed that she had known Brown during his brief stay in the vicinity of the Duck House pub and that before he took leave for the sea he had bitten her on the arm and sucked her blood till he was sated.

The authorities refused to believe the woman, even though she showed them the wound, which was quickly turning gangrenous (and eventually required the amputation of the lower part of that limb). The sailors, however, were another story, and in no time this tale of Brown's vampiristic savagery followed him across the Atlantic where its veracity was never questioned or taken too seriously (as evidenced by its lack of inclusion in press coverage closer to the actual murder and trial itself).

Likewise, there is no contemporaneous record of Brown having actually killed two more individuals during his confinement, and indeed by the time he was transferred to the asylum he was almost fifty years old and suffering from cataracts in both eyes, and obviously debilitated by his life in penal servitude during an era when hard labor meant *very* hard labor. (The Ohio prison he had been transferred to was attached to a rock quarry.)

His transfer to the asylum, however, afforded him a new opportunity. Having been granted commutation by one president, Brown held out hope that he might obtain a full pardon from another. One of these requests reads as follows:

To your Excellency President Cleveland,

. . . When I was called upon by the judge I requested him to postpone my trial until the Bark *Atlantic* returned from sea for these three witnesses [who testified against him] were my enemies for they were not on deck when this occur. They had been sick all the time while they were on board of the *Atlantic* and could not work and the vice consul sent them on with me. Two of them were Portuguese and they could not speak the English language. The judge said to me he cannot postpone my trial because it is too much expense to the government and the Judge would not permit my lawyer to put any questions to these witnesses. . . . Everyone in the court saw that I was shamefully deal most unjustly they all asked to have my sentence remitted from capital sentence to prison for life all desired this because the witnesses were Portuguese sailors and could not speak English therefore their testimony was not sufficient.

Mr. Charles Train my lawyer is dead I have been told by Doctor W.W. Godding and also the Judge and the attorney general who had prosecuted me they are in their graves.

. . . I request of you Your Excellency President Cleveland to give me my release I want to leave the United States.

Your most respectfully James Brown 3th
From the United States of Spanish Columbian Confederation
New Grenada.

Now, Grover Cleveland was by no means a piker when it came to issuing pardons. Over the course of his two terms he issued over eleven hundred of them, including one on September 25, 1894, through a presidential proclamation pardoning Mormons who had previously engaged in polygamous marriages or habitation arrangements including but not limited to such "offenses as bigamy, adultery, polygamy, and unlawful cohabitation (all considered unlawful by the U.S. government)," but to the best of anyone's knowledge or archival record, none were ever issued for the convicted murderer Brown or any alleged vampire Brown.

The story of the allegedly bloodthirsty Mr. Brown would probably have died with him in that asylum had the noted paranormal researcher Charles Fort not stumbled across the *Brooklyn Eagle* article and incorporated it into his often reprinted volume *Wild Talents* as follows:

SOME TIME IN THE year 1867, a fishing smack sailed from Boston. One of the sailors was a Portuguese, who called himself "James Brown." Two of the crew were missing, and were searched for. The captain went into the hold. He held up his lantern, and saw the body of one of these men, in the clutches of "Brown," who was sucking blood from it. Near by was the body of the other sailor. It was bloodless. "Brown" was tried, convicted, and sentenced to be hanged, but President Johnson commuted the sentence to life imprisonment. In October, 1892, the vampire was transferred from the Ohio Penitentiary to the National Asylum, Washington, D.C., and his story was re-told in the newspapers.

. . . thus forever linking in print a U.S. president with a vampire.

The President and the Bodysnatchers
(or rather, Lincoln's "paranormal" exploits as an ex-president)

The assassination of the sixteenth president precipitated a national state of mourning. This included a wide-reaching funeral train with numerous stops to allow the president's body to lay in state in several of the nation's major cities before its interment in Springfield, Illinois, with the intention of its final resting place being part of a carefully designed future monument in Oak Ridge Cemetery.

Unfortunately, a few opportunistic criminals had another idea—but thankfully not the brains and wherewithal to carry it out. This did not keep them from trying, however, for on the night of the presidential election in 1876, a gang of counterfeiters attempted to kidnap the embalmed corpse of the former president with the intention of holding it for ransom.

What follows is an account of this plot based on the interviews that followed:

(From John Carroll Power, ed., *History of an Attempt to Steal the Body of Abraham Lincoln,* Springfield, Ill.: H. W. Rokker, 1890.)

IN 1867, ONLY TWO YEARS after the death of President Lincoln, a lawyer in Springfield, unknown to fame, conceived the brilliant idea of stealing the body of the President, conveying it South, perhaps outside of the United States, secreting it, and waiting for the offer of a ransom, to reveal its place of concealment. He communicated his designs to two young men, one a telegraph operator, the other a mechanic, and tried to induce them to take part with him in the conspiracy. They both declined, and he abandoned the project, most probably because in his offer to them he had furnished witnesses against himself. The lawyer died a few years later. Neither of the young men are living in Springfield now.

But the plot of all plots, for infamy, in conspiring to steal the dead body of a human being, and hold it in concealment, with the hope of extorting ransom money, originated with a man by the name of James B. Kinealy, alias big Jim Kinnelly. He was convicted of having passed a counterfeit fifty dollar note in Peoria, Illinois, and was sentenced to five years in the penitentiary at Joliet. He was serving out that term in 1870, when Elmer Washburn was warden there. At the expiration of his five years, he went to St. Louis, Missouri, and there either really or ostensibly became partner in a livery business. Most likely his livery business was only a cover to other movements. He was in league with expert engravers and printers of counterfeit money. By methods which he seemed to understand well, he organized bands of men at different points, and somehow got into communication with other bands already organized, all of whom he supplied with coney, or bogus money, at a greatly reduced rate, for all the good money they could raise. He would transact business with one only of any given band, and would never permit that one to introduce another of the band, or gang, to him. That one might gather all the good money his gang could raise, go to Kinealy with it, and let him know what was wanted in return. Kinealy would, in a round-about way, go to his engraver and printer and let him know what was wanted, and agree upon a place where it should be deposited, either by a tree or stump, or the corner of a building or fence, in a sewer or under a rock,—any good hiding place, where it never was expected to stay long. He would then return to his visiting patron, get all his good money, take a walk with him, and from a safe distance point out the spot where the bogus money could be found, keep in waiting until his patron obtained it, and gave a previously agreed upon signal that all was right, then each would go his way without coming within speaking distance of each other, until another visit. In this way Kinealy, who was an Irishman by birth, was doing more than any other ten or twenty men to put counterfeit money into circulation, but his natural shrewdness was such, that although his methods were known to detective officers, they could never get a legal hold on him, for he never touched a dollar of bad money.

He was the man who originated the scheme to steal the remains of President Lincoln.

In June, 1876, the Chief of Police for the City of Springfield, Mr. Abner Wilkinson, called the Custodian of the Lincoln Monument aside, while he was walking along the streets, and told him confidentially, that in the discharge of his official duties he had discovered a plot to steal the remains of President Lincoln. The plan, as he understood it, was to take the body from the catacomb at the monument, conceal it in some safe place, and when a sufficient amount of money was offered as a reward for revealing its place of concealment, have some accomplice who could prove himself to have been a long distance away at the time it was taken, find it in a seemingly accidental manner, obtain the reward and divide it among the parties concerned in the scheme. Mr. Wilkinson closed with the suggestion to the Custodian that he should inform the members of the Monument Association, in order to give them an opportunity to take some precautions to guard against the contemplated desecration. Acting on this suggestion the Custodian conveyed the information to Hon. John T. Stuart, Col. John Williams and Jacob Bunn, then the Executive Committee of the National Lincoln Monument Association, and it seemed to them so incredible that no attention was given to it.

The beginning of the Centennial year found a band of thieves and counterfeiters, numbering sixteen men, the names of whom are all in the possession of the writer, with their headquarters at the town bearing the name of our martyred President, Lincoln, the county seat of Logan county, Illinois. It is thirty miles north of Springfield, on the Chicago, Alton and St. Louis Railroad. One of this band has been heard to say, that when in the full tide of their operations, there was more counterfeit than genuine money in circulation in Logan county. Five of that band came to Springfield in March, 1876, rented a store room at the north side of Jefferson street, second door west of Fifth, opened a drinking saloon, and fitted up the room over it for dancing. One of the five was selected as the bartender and was the ostensible proprietor. The others were present by ones and twos, as hangers on. The object of keeping this establishment was that they might be enabled to ply their business of shoving counterfeit money, and use it as a rendezvous where they could, without arousing suspicion, lay their plans to steal the body of President Lincoln. They had frequent meetings, each and all visited the monument, mingled with other visitors, and one and another would ask such questions as would bring out all the facts about the different enclosures of the body, including the sarcophagus, as would be important for them to know. Early in June every detail was arranged, and the night of July 3, 1876, agreed upon as the time for putting their diabolical designs into execution. They were to open the marble sarcophagus, and take the body in the leaden and wood coffins, convey all to the Sangamon river about two miles north, and bury it in a gravel bar under a bridge, then disperse and wait for a reward, or an opportunity to negotiate for its return.

The time was chosen with demoniac shrewdness. The miscreants judged that, on the morning of July 4th, while the people in every part of our nation, with the most elaborate preparations, were in the very act of giving expression to a hundred years of self-sacrificing patriotism, in founding and perfecting a system of government under which all men are free, to have the news conveyed to them by lightning flashes, that the remains of the beloved central figure, in the crowning act, had been ignominiously torn from their resting place in the stately Mausoleum erected for the purpose, by the people, would call forth fabulous sums of money, as free-will offerings, that they might be rescued from vandal hands.

But Satan sometimes furnishes the means to defeat his best laid schemes, and thus overleaps himself, and this was one of such occasions. Gen. Peter Horry, of South Carolina, a local historian of the American Revolution, makes use of the following language: "That great poet, John Milton, who seems to have known him well, assures us that the devil was the inventor of gunpowder. But, for my own part, were I in the humor to ascribe any particular invention to the author of all evil, it should be that of distilling apple brandy. We have Scripture for it that he began his capers with the apple; then, why not go on with the brandy, which is but the fiery juice of the apple."

Gen. Horry then relates a number of instances of the disastrous effects of intoxicating drinks among the soldiers who achieved our independence, closing with one in which it accidentally did good by preventing a battle between two parties of patriots. This makes it in order here to relate how whisky defeated the best laid scheme ever devised, by the conspirators, to steal the remains of President Lincoln.

When their preparations were all complete, there were two or three weeks' time to while away in idleness, while waiting for the night of July 3rd. This was the most trying point.

Until that time, all had gone along smoothly, for each and all had kept their secrets, and not a shadow of suspicion had been aroused. During this period of waiting, one of the five who came to Springfield in March and opened the saloon, a man of more intelligence than either of the other four, or all of them combined, but of exceedingly depraved morals, became elated as he mentally dwelt upon the prospect of the great wealth they expected to obtain as a reward for giving up the remains or revealing the place of their concealment, took on board an unusual quantity of whisky, went around among the women of the town, and confidentially told one of the keepers of a house of ill-repute that he was in a conspiracy to "steal old Lincoln's bones," and would by that means extort so much money from some source, of which he did not seem to have any definite idea, as a reward for giving up their secrets, that they would all be rich, and would expect her and her friends to help them spend the money.

It was through this channel that Chief of Police Wilkinson obtained the information he gave to the Custodian of the Monument, as already stated. The man who divulged the secret was the editor of a political paper at Lincoln. He left Springfield while he was yet intoxicated, but returning in a few days sober, found that the free use of his tongue when drunk, had defeated the whole scheme. The contents of the saloon were soon after loaded into wagons and driven away in the middle of the night, leaving a rent bill unpaid. Whisky alone is entitled to the credit of having thwarted this well-laid scheme to steal the remains of President Lincoln, but the fact that there was such a scheme did not at the time become generally known, and the half suppressed rumors of it gained but little credence with those who heard it.

Those sixteen men, shoving counterfeit money in the town of Lincoln and Logan county, constituted one of Kinealy's bands. After perfecting the scheme in his own mind, he communicated it to the messenger, who acted between him and the band, when the messenger was on one of his trips to St. Louis, to exchange good for bad money; and entrusted that messenger with the execution of the plot. It was he, with four others whom he had selected from the sixteen, who came to Springfield, in March, 1876, and opened the drinking saloon and dancing room.

After the plot was divulged by the drunkenness of one of their number, in June, Kinealy had nothing more to do with any of the Logan county band, and for a time disappeared from their sight.

[At this point Powers supplements his account with a letter that fills in some of the details about how the conspiracy was not at this point curtailed, but merely delayed.]

I next wrote direct to the writer of the above, and received the following reply:

GE county, Kansas, April, 1887.

J. C. Power, Springfield, Ill.:

DEAR SIR. Yours, with reference to the plot to steal the remains of President Lincoln, is received. The information obtained by me was from BS, while under the influence of intoxicating liquor. At the time I did not attach much importance to his statements, but thought it was only the vaporings of a drunken man. After the attempt was actually made, I, in conversation, told M.S.W. that I could find the guilty parties. He at once put himself in com- munication with the authorities, but the arrest of the criminals followed so quickly after the attempt that I came to the belief that BS and his gang had organized for the purpose stated, but had been forestalled by the Chicago band. The plan as detailed to me was, that a party of five or six was to go to Springfield with a strong spring wagon, just a day's drive from our place, thirty miles, stay in the city until after dark, then drive to the cemetery, make an entrance into the grounds at the nearest point to the Monument, drive to the foot of the hill on which it stands, leaving one of their number to watch the team.

The others would go to the Monument, break it open, get
the casket containing the body, carry it to the wagon and
drive away, he saying that it would be impossible to track
them very far on the sandy roads, across the Sangamon
river bottoms, on which the line of flight was planned. He
further stated that they would be a long distance from
Springfield before morning, and would have the body
deposited in a secure hiding place, where they would defy
any one to find it. There it was to remain until the reward,
which they believed would be offered, should be large
enough to satisfy the gang. Then it was to be discovered
by a reputable farmer, by the name of MC, who was
related to BS by marriage.

The wagon proposed to be used on the trip belonged to MC. He is a good man, respected by all who
know him; was a strong Lincoln man; served three years
in the Thirty-second Illinois Infantry. I do not think the
project was ever mentioned to him. He would not have
consented to be concerned in any such undertaking. I feel
sure that BS did not tell me where the body was to be
concealed, but intimated that the place was not far away. I
have since found the place, I am confident. BS lived about
two miles west of MC, and three-fourths of a mile west
of old Yankeetown, in a small frame house, one-quarter
of a mile south of the wagon road leading from C to Mt.
Pulaski. The place of concealment was under this house.
BS had dug a pit, or cellar, three and a half feet wide,
seven or eight feet long, and two and a half to three feet
deep. The pit was dug secretly, no one having any knowledge of the time or manner, nor noticed any fresh earth
about the place. It is thought that it was dug at night
and the earth taken and dropped into a small stream of

running water that flowed near the house. There was a long door constructed in the floor of the house over the pit, not having any hinges or ring by which to open it, and while BS occupied the house, this door was always covered by a long strip of carpet, the other parts of the floor being bare. There was no necessity for digging a cellar under the house, as there was a good one outside, and there being no conveniences for opening and closing the door showed that it was not intended for daily use. BS also told one GD, who, I am confident, belonged to the Logan county counterfeiting gang, of the plot to steal Mr. Lincoln's body, and he (GD) told it to WHD, a merchant of C, who communicated the same to Fox & House, hardware merchants of Springfield, they agreeing to put the proper ones on their guard. Now, as to the dates, I am all at sea. I know it was in the fall of 1876, and only a short time before the attempt was made, that BS and I had the talk. I am of the opinion that there were two or three plots; I think, three. The one with which BS was connected was composed of Logan county crooks, some of the men whose names you sent me being in frequent consultation with him, also some whose names you do not mention, namely, GD, already spoken of, JHP and MS, cousins of BS. This is all I remember now. If there is anything further you wish to know, or any questions you wish to ask as to anything I have written, ask, and I will answer as best I can. The long time elapsed since the events has caused my memory to lose many of the details, of which I was cognizant at the time. Thanks for the list of names of the counterfeiters. I was acquainted with many of them.

Respectfully, G.K.K.

[Powers returns to his narrative.]

In the absence of Tyrrell from Chicago, Swegles, after obtaining the information related in the preceding pages about the conspiracy, consulted an attorney, C. W. Dean, without giving the names of the conspirators, and was advised by Dean to lay all the facts before Tyrrell on his arrival. In the meantime Dean informed Hon. Leonard Swett and Robert T. Lincoln of what was being done. On the arrival of Tyrrell, Swegles unfolded to him the scheme, as far as it had come to his knowledge. He said that a party or parties from St. Louis had been in consultation at a drinking saloon called the "Hub," at 294 West Madison street, with Terrence Mullen, the proprietor, one Jack Hughes, alias Shepherd, and a well known contractor of Chicago. They were all to meet at Springfield early some evening, steal the body, place it in a light, strong spring wagon, prepared by the con- tractor, who was to drive with all possible speed, by the aid of relays of horses previously arranged, to the sand hills in the northern part of Indiana, and bury it where the moving sand, caused by the winds, would soon obliterate all evidences of their thirty-ninth anniversary of the assignation of Rev. Elijah P. Lovejoy, the first prominent mar- tyr in the cause of abolishing human slavery in the United States of America, which occurred at Alton, Illinois, about the same hour on the evening of Nov. 7, 1837.

Many visitors have expressed surprise that the marble was not broken. Swegles explained that to the writer, when he was here the next May at the trial. He said they found no difficulty in removing the extreme top piece, but when they attempted to remove the main lid, which projects over the sides, it was found that although the cement was broken, they could not turn it around. Mullins was in the act of striking upward with the axe, to break off the edges of the projecting marble, when Swegles caught his arm and reminded him that it was but a short distance to the residence of the sexton of the Cemetery; and that they might be heard and compelled to leave without accomplishing their object. He then proposed that they all join in removing it, which they did by lifting until the fact was revealed that there were three copper dowels on each side. By lifting it above these dowels, they were able to turn it across the sarcophagus, when they pushed it back against the wall.

When we all went from the Monument into the city, some visited the telegraph and newspaper offices, and an account of the events of the evening was read next morning, not only in the papers of our own country, but in all other countries reached by the telegraph, producing a sensation which for a time overshadowed the election news. Tyrrell, Hay and McDonald boarded the midnight train on the Chicago and Alton road for Chicago. Swegles went on the same train, but kept as much under cover as possible. Washburn and McGinn remained to examine the field next morning. There was some expectation that Hughes and Mullins would also go on the midnight train for Chicago, but they were too shrewd for that. The next morning they called for breakfast at a farm house north of the Sangamon river, about seven miles northeast of Springfield, and after that disappeared for nearly ten days, when Swegles reported to Tyrrell that they were together at the "Hub," Mullins' drinking saloon 294 West Madison street, Chicago. A warrant was procured and placed in the hands of Dennis Simms, of the Chicago city police force.

About eleven o'clock on the evening of Nov. 17, 1876, officers Simms, McGinn, Tyrrell and ex-Chief Washburn entered the "Hub," and at the same time captured both Mullins and Hughes, handcuffed them, drove to the Central police station and lodged them in prison. They were brought to Springfield, arriving on the Chicago and Alton train, Saturday morning, Nov. 18th. They were visited at the county jail and identified by several persons, the Custodian among them, who had seen them while here on their ghoulish expedition.

. . . It was so much easier to dispose of the whole question of the Lincoln tomb robbery by crying "put up job," on the part of the detectives, than to investigate the subject and obtain the facts, that charges of that kind were freely made, and rung on all the changes up and down the scale. They especially charged that the plot was gotten up in the interest of Elmer Washburn, who had until a short time previous to that event been Chief of the United States Secret Service. A letter from Hon. Leonard Swett, in the *Chicago Tribune* of Nov. 23, 1876, very emphatically refutes that charge, and I think in justice to him that it should form a part of this history.

The letter is as follows:

CHICAGO, Nov. 22 (1876). As intimations have been made in the daily papers that the arrest of the parties charged with desecrating the tomb of Abraham Lincoln was fraudulent, and induced by Elmer Washburn, and as the facts of his connection with the case are known to me, and based upon my request, I consider it my duty, in justice to him, and without his knowledge or solicitation, to state what I know in reference to the facts involved.

One day during the Sullivan trial, a lawyer came to me manifesting great earnestness, and said a client of his had revealed to him the fact that a plan was on foot to steal the body of Abraham Lincoln. I do not consider it proper to state anything more in reference to this plan or its objects, than to say that it had no connection with politics, but was simply crime, and to accomplish criminal and mercenary ends.

I asked permission to state the facts to Robert Lincoln, and upon consultation with him wrote to John T. Stuart, of Springfield, who had been prominently connected with the Lincoln Monument Association, stating simply what I had heard, and expressed no opinion upon the facts, but suggested that perhaps the slightest intimation of danger ought to induce proper safeguards, if the body was in a position where it could possibly be exposed to such a scheme. The next day brought to my knowledge the fact that any public guard, or open precaution would simply postpone the attempt, and therefore, upon the belief that the officers themselves would catch the parties in the act, it was thought best to let them do it.

I therefore wrote to Mr. Stuart again, telling him that the plan had been matured to catch the perpetrators in the act, but while this was promised, and in deference to it our precautions should be secret, still they should be so effectual as to leave no danger of the success of the thieves. Some ten days elapsed, the details of which I purposely omit, but the result was that the parties got ready and selected election night, because public attention would then be absorbed.

Up to this time, all I had done was at the request of Robert Lincoln, to induce the precautions at Springfield above stated. He also asked me, as he did not wish to act in the matter, to do anything I might consider prudent and proper. He came to me the day of the night the parties were going, and said he was fearful generally about what would be done, and the result, and I suggested, as Elmer Washburn was in town, and I placed full reliance both in his discretion and integrity, that we should consult him generally on the situation.

That afternoon Mr. Washburn was consulted by Robert, but I was not able to be present, and that night after this consultation, Mr. Washburn informed me that the parties had gone to Springfield on the evening train. This was the first information I had that they were going at a definite time, or that they had gone. If I had known certainly that they were going, I should have procured Washburn to follow them at once, but then it was too late.

I begged Washburn to go down the next morning, but he expressed reluctance because he had no authority, and it might seem like interfering. I told him I was authorized by Robert to act, and urged him in every way I could to go to Springfield on the morning train. He finally promised that, after voting at the Twenty-second Street Station, he would then take the Chicago and Alton train if he could, and if he failed he would report to me, and I said I would get a special engine for him.

After leaving him I became fearful, that in thinking the matter over his disinclination to interfere might finally prevail, and I went to Twenty-second Street Station a few minutes after the polls opened and waited until nine, for the purpose of placing in his hands a written request on behalf of Robert and myself for him to take charge of the matter in connection with Mr. Tyrrell.

Missing him there, as he, in fact, voted near the Palmer House, I went to Roberts' house, and after becoming satisfied that he had gone on the nine o'clock train, we telegraphed him at Bloomington, en route, to take charge of the matter, and we would back him in whatever he might do. The object of this was that he might feel authorized to act, as far as we could authorize him. That night Washburn telegraphed me that the parties had escaped, but although temporarily baffled, he and Mr. Tyrrell worked with skill and caution, and finally caught the men.

Nobody in connection with this whole matter has been trying to make any money or affix any conditions to their work, or in any way secure any compensation. The only money that has been paid out is a matter of $2.00

per day to some parties connected with the case who are poor and could not give their time without compensation.

The conduct of the officers has been such as would meet with the approval of all, provided they knew the facts involved. The arrests having been made, I employed the Hon. Charles H. Reed to go to Springfield to take charge of the prosecution.

I did this because I thought my feelings might misguide me, and I knew him to be one of the best prosecutors in the country. When all the facts are known, the gentlemen I have named will be entitled to, and doubtless will receive, the thanks of all who loved Mr. Lincoln and who wish that his ashes may rest in peace.

Yours truly,

LEONARD SWETT.

The capture of these miscreants brought about a remarkable revelation. The reader will remember that James B. Kinealy, who originated in St. Louis the first plot to rob the tomb of Lincoln, put it into the hands of a go-between, or messenger between himself and his band of coney men at the town of Lincoln, Logan county, Illinois, to carry into execution. The messenger selecting four others, they five came to Springfield, and when all things were about ready to consummate their designs, the drunkenness of one of their number exploded the scheme, and Kinealy went under cover, and was seen no more by officers until after the arrest of Hughes and Mullins, when it was found that he was partner with Mullins in the "Hub" saloon. He was the party from St. Louis mentioned by Swegles in his reports to Tyrrell of his first interviews with the conspirators. The officers then having no charge against Kinealy, he was left there. His good fortune or natural shrewdness seems afterward to have forsaken him.

He was arrested in St. Louis, Missouri, April 14, 1880, for dealing and having in his possession counterfeit $10 U.S. Treasury notes, and Nov. 18, 1882, he plead guilty in the U.S. District Court in St. Louis, and was sentenced to serve one year in Chester, Illinois, penitentiary, and he served that term.

At that time there was not a law on the statute books of Illinois that made it a penitentiary offense to rob a grave or in any way steal a dead body. A law was enacted and approved May 21, 1879, which came in force July first of the same year, under which a party convicted of that offense, is subject to a penalty of not less than one nor more than ten years in the penitentiary. In order to inflict anything like an adequate penalty, these men had to be tried for something more than an attempt to steal the remains of President Lincoln. The circuit court of Sangamon county was in session at the time they were captured, but its grand jury for that term had transacted all the business that came before it, and had been discharged. This case was so shocking to the finer feelings of humanity that it was thought by the court to be of sufficient importance to summon a special grand jury, to proceed with the case at once, and it was accordingly done.

Even though Lincoln's body seems to have been allowed to remain at rest (and indeed well protected from that point onward), there have been numerous accounts of his spirit being seen wandering around the White House grounds with many sightings near the room where the so-called Lincoln bed is kept.

Many of these Lincoln sightings are generic in nature, but the following occurrences have all been cited or mentioned on more than one occasion:

- A bodyguard to President Benjamin Harrison claimed that he had to serve extra duty because the Civil War–veteran president was disturbed by mysterious footsteps in the hall outside his bedchamber. The president supposedly ascribed these sounds to his former commander in chief during the war, and it is alleged that the guard eventually attended a séance to beg President Lincoln to stop so he could get enough sleep to properly protect the president.

- A twentieth-century White House staff member claimed to have seen Lincoln sitting on his bed pulling on his boots.

- Presidents Theodore Roosevelt, Herbert Hoover, and Harry Truman all reported hearing unexplained rappings on their bedroom doors and allegedly attributed them to the spirit of the former president.

- Calvin Coolidge's wife reported seeing on several occasions the ghost of Lincoln standing with his hands clasped behind his back, at a window in the Oval Office, staring out in deep contemplation in the direction of the bloody battlefields across the Potomac. The "ghost" did not interact with First Lady Coolidge and may not have been an actual "presence" but rather a vestigial memory of a scene from the past that she just happened to be sensitive to.

- Eleanor Roosevelt used the former Lincoln bedroom as her study during her tenure as First Lady and often spoke of the feeling that she was being watched by someone who may or may not have been corporeal in nature. Many have attributed this as a Lincoln sighting, though there is no record that Eleanor ever came to that conclusion.

- Also during the Roosevelt administration, on a state visit Queen Wilhelmina of the Netherlands was supposedly awakened by a knock on the bedroom door only to be confronted with the ghost of Abe Lincoln staring at her from the hallway.

- There is also rumor that the former president appeared to Prime Minister Winston Churchill during one of his White House stays. As the story goes, Churchill had just finished a bath and a hot toddy while enjoying a robust cigar, and upon leaving the tub was confronted by the ghost of the former president. It is alleged that the prime minister said, "Good evening, Mr. President. You seem to have me at a disadvantage," and that the ghost smiled and disappeared. It is noteworthy that this incident does not appear in any of Churchill's own memoirs.

Chapter 12

The Unsettling Coincidences of Jinxy McDeath

In a 1909 letter to Richard Watson Gilder, editor of *The Century Magazine*, Robert Lincoln verified the following episode, which occurred while his father was president:

THE INCIDENT OCCURRED WHILE a group of passengers were late at night purchasing their sleeping car places from the conductor who stood on the station platform at the entrance of the car. The platform was about the height of the car floor, and there was of course a narrow space between the platform and the car body. There was some crowding, and I happened to be pressed by it against the car body while waiting my turn. In this situation the train began to move, and by the motion I was twisted off my feet, and had dropped somewhat, with feet downward, into the open space, and was personally helpless, when my coat collar was vigorously seized and I was quickly pulled up and out to a secure footing on the platform. Upon turning to thank my rescuer I saw it was Edwin Booth, whose face was of course well known to me, and I expressed my gratitude to him, and in doing so, called him by name.

Months after the incident, in 1865, Booth received a letter from a friend, Colonel Adam Badeau, then serving as an officer on Grant's staff. Lincoln had related the story of the rescue to Badeau while they were stationed at City Point, Va., and Badeau supposedly offered Booth his compliments for having performed such a deed.

Having been saved by the brother of the man who would soon assassinate his father is more than a bit unsettling. This, however, was not the only coincidence in the life of the president's son, or the most unnerving.

Indeed, Robert Lincoln's life was far from enviable. He experienced the hardships of Civil War combat as a captain on General Ulysses S. Grant's staff and was partially estranged from his father (who preferred Robert's brothers, Willie and Tad, who died young; Robert was the only of the president's sons to survive to adulthood). Eventually he had to commit his mother, Mary Todd Lincoln, to a psychiatric hospital and take charge of her finances as well, due to her careless and spendthrift ways.

However, probably the gravest burden he bore was as a proximate witness to not one but all three of the successful assassinations of a U.S. president during his lifetime. For this statistically anomalous experience, author Sara Vowell in her marvelous book *Assassination Vacation* (the best and most entertaining book on American presidential assassinations ever written, and perhaps the smartest book of pop history in recent years) dubbed the presidential scion with the moniker Jinxy McDeath, a rather accurate nickname given his dubious honor.

In April of 1865, Robert had just returned to Washington, D.C., after having witnessed Grant's immortal sit-down with Robert E. Lee at Appomattox Courthouse on April 9. Indeed, he was likely still worn out from his stint at Grant's side, which was probably the only reason he declined his parents' invitation to accompany them to the performance of *Our American Cousin* at Ford's Theater that infamous night, preferring to remain at the White House residence a few blocks away. Word reached him around midnight that his father had been shot, and he hastened to the president's bedside at the Peterson house (across the street from the theater), where his father eventually expired.

After the events of the presidential funeral, Robert and his mother moved back to Illinois, where he completed his law school education. He returned to Washington a few years later to accept an appointment as James Garfield's secretary of war in 1881.

It was probably due to his Cabinet position that Robert found himself at the Sixth Street Train Station in Washington, D.C., on July 2, 1881, as per a personal invitation from the president himself. The president was on his way to his alma mater, Williams College in Massachusetts, to deliver a speech and desired the companionship of his secretary of state and secretary of war.

It was on this date and at that place that Garfield was shot by the disgruntled Charles Guiteau, who had been unsuccessful petitioning the president for a civil service appointment. One bullet grazed Garfield's arm; the second bullet lodged in his spine and could not be found (although scientists today think that the bullet was near his lung), and Robert was by his side as the shooting went down. Garfield died from his wounds and subsequent complications eighty days later.

Robert served out the rest of his tenure as secretary of war under Garfield's successor, President Chester A. Arthur, and then returned to the private sector with the exception of a short stint as U.S. ambassador to England during the Benjamin Harrison administration (safely an ocean away from the proximity of the commander in chief).

After his diplomatic stint, Robert accepted a position on the board of the Pullman Palace Car Company as general counsel. It was in this capacity he was attending the Pan American Exposition in Buffalo, New York, on September 6, 1901, as a personal guest of President William McKinley, who at the Temple of Music exhibit was greeting the public until 4:07 p.m. Leon Czolgosz fired twice at the president, grazing his shoulder and hitting him in the abdomen. Robert was just in the process of detraining in Buffalo when word of the assault reached him. The twenty-fifth president died eight days later from complications from his gunshot wounds.

For Robert Todd Lincoln: three invitations, three dead presidents.

Robert lived twenty-five more years after the McKinley incident, and one can easily assume that he found himself the recipient of far fewer presidential invitations over the rest of his life, as commanders in chief can never be too careful.

Chapter 13

The Twentieth-Century
Presidents and Their Seers

With the advent of the twentieth century and the threat of so-called world wars, one might imagine that the occupants of 1600 Pennsylvania Avenue would have turned their focus away from séances and spiritualism. Instead they might have embraced a more pragmatic and less occult means for discerning the best course of action for national matters of great import and personal matters of great turmoil.

Indeed, the 1912 election of Woodrow Wilson as the twenty-eighth president signaled a new move toward intellectualism over populism in the politics of the nation, as Wilson was the first president to have earned a doctorate. Yet such credentials did not necessarily indicate a lack of willingness to embrace the unknown.

Edgar Cayce

According to Woodrow Wilson's White House biography:

AFTER GRADUATION FROM PRINCETON (then the College of New Jersey) and the University of Virginia Law School, Wilson earned his doctorate at Johns Hopkins University and entered upon an academic career. In 1885 he married Ellen Louise Axson.

Wilson advanced rapidly as a conservative young professor of political science and became president of Princeton in 1902.

His growing national reputation led some conservative Democrats to consider him Presidential timber. . . . After the Germans signed the Armistice in November 1918, Wilson went to Paris to try to build an enduring peace. He later presented to the Senate the Versailles Treaty, containing the Covenant of the League of Nations, and asked, "Dare we reject it and break the heart of the world?" But the election of 1918 had shifted the balance in Congress to the Republicans. By seven votes the Versailles Treaty failed in the Senate. The President, against the warnings of his doctors, had made a national tour to mobilize public sentiment for the treaty. Exhausted, he suffered a stroke and nearly died. Tenderly nursed by his second wife, Edith Bolling Galt, he lived until 1924.

When confronted with his own mortality by his October 2, 1919, stroke (and subsequent incapacitation), one finds more than a bit of evidence that the president sought out the counsel of a now well-known mystic by the name of Edgar Cayce.

Cayce's bio from the organization he helped found (the Association for Research and Enlightenment, or ARE) reads as follows:

FOR FORTY-THREE YEARS OF his adult life, Edgar Cayce demonstrated the uncanny ability to put himself into some kind of self-induced sleep state by lying down on a couch, closing his eyes, and folding his hands over his stomach. This state of relaxation and meditation enabled him to place his mind in contact with all time and space. From this state he could respond to questions as diverse as "What are the secrets of the universe?" to "How can I remove a wart?" His responses to these questions came to be called "readings" and contain insights so valuable that even to this day individuals have found practical help for everything from maintaining a well-balanced diet and improving human relationships to overcoming life-threatening illnesses and experiencing a closer walk with God.

Cayce (1877–1945) was sometimes known as the Sleeping Prophet and wrote numerous books during his lifetime, and even more voluminous volumes after his death based on his uncollected writings. He is considered to be the spiritual forerunner of the New Age movement for his mystical studies and predictions, medical clairvoyance, and scientific insights. His predictions included the failure of Prohibition, the stock market crash, the first and second world wars, and the deaths of two presidents. The idea of a U.S. president seeking his counsel is more than a bit odd, which accounts for the surreptitious nature of the alleged meeting (which was in character for the incapacitated president, who managed to hide the full depth of his medical problems from his Cabinet and vice president to avoid the possibility of being relieved of his office, as specified in the Constitution).

In *Edgar Cayce—My Life as a Seer: The Lost Memoirs,* Cayce confidante David Kahn recalled, "At one time we were asked to give a reading on President Woodrow Wilson.... I believe this was during the time he was in the wheelchair and incapacitated and Mrs. Wilson was looking after his affairs. My recollection was that Colonel Starling (of the Secret Service) arranged this reading as he was a lifelong friend of Edgar Cayce."

Kahn did not claim to witness the reading nor did he claim to be aware of its exact nature, though one might infer that given Wilson's condition it might have been one of Cayce's so-called medical readings. According to Sidney D. Kirkpatrick's critical (and unauthorized but well-documented) biography *Edgar Cayce—An American Prophet*:

HOWEVER EASY IT MIGHT be to dismiss Kahn's claims as mere speculation, there is much evidence connecting Cayce to President Wilson, much of it involving Edgar's well documented friendship with Major Alfred M. Wilson and his brother

Major Edwin G. Wilson from Franklin, Pennsylvania, both first cousins of the President, whom Cayce came to know through one of his Selma Bible students, and who would receive and conduct numerous readings after the war. Their confidence in Cayce was unshakable, as evidenced by numerous letters in the Cayce archive.

A second potential connection between Edgar, and the President was through Cayce's friendship with Colonel Will Starling, the star pitcher on the Hopkinsville Moguls who became a member of the Secret Service detail assigned to protect the President during the war years. . . . Like the President's cousins Alfred and Edwin, Starling would also receive readings from Cayce and become quite an outspoken champion of his abilities.

Apart from these connections, there is the fact that Cayce—in trance—frequently discussed the formation of the League of Nations and how crucial it was that the President gain the support and confidence of the American people in his endeavor to ratify the peace treaty. In these readings, poetic in their delivery and prophetic in their message, Cayce clearly suggested future problems and another "great war" that might come as a result of the failure by the United States to support the President.

Kirkpatrick further quotes Kahn: "I did not see the reading given, but as I understand, it described the President's condition and foretold that his time was limited and he would not get well."

Wilson did manage to live out his presidency but never did succeed in getting the League of Nations ratified or bouncing back from the stroke. After officially leaving office he lived in a Washington, D.C., residence located at 2340 S Street Northwest, just off Embassy Row. He died there quietly in February 1924, though a 1969 article in the *Washington Post* suggests that his postdeath experience is far from quiet, according to a former caretaker who claims to still hear his shuffling, cane-supported walk in various locales of the old house, and no less an expert than the paranormal investigator Hans Holzer claims to have possibly conversed with his spiritual presence with the assistance of a medium in his book *White House Ghosts*.

Jeane Dixon

Jeane Dixon was born in Medford, Wisconsin, in 1904 and supposedly had her first psychic experience when she was a child barely old enough to talk. Dixon the toddler asked her mother if she could play with a curious-looking letter, which was to arrive several days later. Unlike many of her occult contemporaries, Dixon attributed her abilities as being a gift from God and often correlated her astrological studies with Christian concepts (such as relating the signs of the zodiac with the attributes of the twelve original apostles). She later predicted the tragic fates of several celebrities with astonishing accuracy (at least according to her acolytes) and at the time of her death was still writing a column that was syndicated in over eight hundred daily newspapers worldwide.

Tabloid astrologers and celebrity mystics were still a dime a dozen in the fifties, but with a certain "presidential prediction" Dixon quickly shot to the head of the pack in terms of prominence.

The May 13, 1956, issue of *Parade* magazine contains an article that reads in part: "As for the 1960 election, Mrs. Dixon thinks it will be dominated by labor and won by a Democrat. But he will be assassinated or die in office, though not necessarily in his first term." And, as related in her 1997 obituary, "After Kennedy's death in 1963, the national notice that Dixon received led political columnist Ruth Montgomery to write a book, *A Gift of Prophecy: The Phenomenal Jeane Dixon*, that recounted hundreds of accurate predictions made over the years. The book, published in 1965, sold more than 3 million copies and brought Dixon even more demand on the lecture circuit and a syndicated horoscope column."

In her 1969 memoir, *My Life and Prophecies*, she summed up the purpose of her gift in an author's note, which read: "The purpose of this book is to show that as God spoke through the prophets so does He convey a message through each of us. And that message is that each one of us has an individual purpose to fulfill in His Divine Plan."

Dixon became a talk-show celebrity, a quiz-show favorite, and a tabloid darling with her many predictions, but few would ever have suspected the ears in high places that hung on her every word.

A 2007 article in *Newsweek* by Michael Isikoff, based on transcripts of Richard Nixon's tapes, and research from historian Timothy Naftali details that the Nixon White House had an unofficial psychic adviser in Dixon, thanks to her relationship with the president's private secretary, Rose Mary Woods (of "erased tape" fame). Nixon referred to Dixon as "the soothsayer" and Woods would relay to him briefings from her on national security forecasts.

According to the article:

"In what University of Virginia historian and 9/11 Commission researcher Timothy Naftali calls 'one of the oddest moments in the history of U.S. counterterrorism,' Woods alerted Nixon to some of Dixon's most alarming warnings during an Oval Office meeting that took place September 19, 1972, between 3:27 p.m. and 3:42 p.m. This meeting (which has never previously been detailed) took place just two weeks after nine Israeli Olympic athletes kidnapped by Palestinian terrorists were killed during a botched rescue attempt by West German authorities.

" 'There are going to be killings here in America, bombing of Jews,' Woods told the president, explaining she had just been told this in a recent session she had with Dixon. The psychic (who at the time wrote a newspaper astrology column) warned that Jewish leaders were going 'to commence attacks on you [Nixon] for not protecting them,' according to Woods's briefing. But she said Dixon was concerned for the president—and advised him not to 'say something.'"

The subject of Dixon's prophecies returned to the Oval Office two days later when Nixon met with Henry Kissinger to discuss the terrorism threat. "Rose talks to this soothsayer, Jeane Dixon, all the time," Nixon told Kissinger, according to a tape of the September 21, 1972, meeting. "They are desperate that [the terrorists] will kidnap somebody. They may shoot somebody. We have got to have a plan. Suppose they do, for example, Henry, suppose they kidnap [Yitzhak] Rabin? And they ask us to release all blacks who are prisoners around the United States. And we didn't and they shoot him? Think of it! What the Christ do we do? We are not going to give into it. We have got to have contingency plans for hijacking, for kidnapping, for all sorts of things that can happen around here."

The official White House records indicate that the president had at least one documented Oval Office meeting directly with Dixon—a thirty-six-minute session on May 4, 1971. But his was not the only administration to seek the counsel of the noted astrologer as a close confidante; another California-based presidential contender was also among those she counseled.

According to eighty-seven-year-old Leo M. Bernstein, curator of the Jeane Dixon Museum and Library, in a 2002 interview with the *Washington Post*, "Dixon's highest-profile client was former First Lady Nancy Reagan, who once felt—no matter how mercilessly the media dogged her for it—that no important life decision should be made without Dixon's consultation. It also helped that, in 1962, Dixon told Ronald Reagan that he would one day hold the highest public office in the United States. President Reagan wouldn't get on a plane until Dixon told Nancy it was okay."

At a certain point, however, Dixon fell out of vogue, and though her following among the masses increased dramatically through her tabloid exposure and the media attention provided by such outlets as the *National Enquirer* and the *Star* (as well as her syndicated daily column), her circle of celebrity clients began to dwindle. One such case was indeed the former First Lady of California, who was soon taking up residence at the White House with a hotline to a new astrologer in tow.

Joan Quigley

One of the endearing qualities about Ronald Reagan was that he was an everyman sort of guy, unencumbered by the details and minutiae of politics. Several of his staffers (before and after his election as the fortieth president) used to mention that at home on the ranch Ronald Reagan was the sort of man who read his horoscope and the "funnies" before the rest of the paper. In the words of his daughter Patti (in her memoir, *The Way I See It*), "I'd heard my parents read their horoscopes aloud at the breakfast table, but that seemed pretty innocuous to me. Occasionally, I read mine, too—usually so I can do the exact opposite of what it says . . . but my parents have done what the stars suggested—altered schedules, changed travel plans, stayed home, cancelled appearances."

Whether Ronald Reagan actually took the horoscopes he read in the papers seriously is up for debate, but the fact that his wife, Nancy, took them as seriously as life and death has been confirmed by a wide variety of sources.

Nancy always valued her relationship with her astrologer and preferred personal attention beyond that afforded by a general column in the newspapers, so when she and Jeane Dixon drifted apart, with Nancy dissatisfied at her lack of personal attention and a vague sense that "Jeane may have lost her powers," the soon-to-be First Lady sought out a replacement. Sometime during the seventies, Nancy was introduced to Joan Quigley by her friend talk-show host and producer Merv Griffin.

Joan Quigley was a San Francisco horoscope expert who considered astrology a science, related to astronomy, and made more precise by the discovery of modern planets. (Quigley believes that astrology is not related to paranormal abilities, and she has never claimed to be psychic.) The approved jacket copy of her autobiography, *What Does Joan Say? My Seven Years as White House Astrologer to Nancy and Ronald Reagan,* reads as follows:

"Never in the history of the U.S. Presidency has an astrologer played such a significant role in a nation's affairs of State. Quigley wielded considerable influence in the creation of major U.S. policy, including the Bitburg crisis, the INF Treaty, and the President's historical shift from viewing Russia as the Evil Empire to accepting Gorbachev as a peace-seeking leader."

That said, and hyperbole aside, there is indeed little doubt that she exerted a significant influence on the Reagan White House once she succeeded Jeane Dixon as the preferred seer. After the first assassination attempt on Ronald Reagan's life, Merv Griffin allegedly told the First Lady that Quigley had mentioned to him that she could have predicted based on the president's chart that that date may have been fraught with peril for her husband. As sources later revealed, Nancy immediately contacted Quigley, establishing a hotline at both the White House and Camp David to reach her in case she saw something in the charts for her or her husband.

Eventually all of the president's scheduled appointments were cross-referenced with charts Quigley drew up in advance, such as:

Late Dec thru March *bad*

Jan 16–23 *very bad*

Jan 20 *nothing outside White House—possible attempt*

Feb 20–26 *be careful*

March 7–14 *bad period*

March 10–14 *no outside activity!*

March 16 *very bad*

March 21 *no*

March 27 *no*

March 12–19 *no trips exposure*

March 19–25 *no public exposure*

April 3 *careful*

April 11 *careful*

April 17 *careful*

April 21–28 *stay home*

... much to the dismay of many on the fortieth president's staff who were less than pleased at having their schedules impacted by a so-called stargazer.

Upon leaving office, Reagan's former chief of staff, Donald Regan, having had numerous clashes with the First Lady, made the White House's special relationship with an astrologer quite public in his hastily put-together tell-all memoir, *For the Record: From Wall Street to Washington.*

According to Regan:

"Mrs. Reagan passed along her prognostications to me after conferring on the telephone—she had become such a factor in my work, and in the highest affairs of the nation, that at one point I kept a color-coded calendar on my desk (numerals highlighted in green ink for "good" days, red for "bad" days, yellow for "iffy" days) as an aid to remembering when it was propitious to move the President of the United States from one place to another, or schedule him to speak in public, or commence negotiations with a foreign power.... Obviously this list of dangerous or forbidden dates left very little latitude for scheduling."

Regan was more than willing to give voice to the absurdity of the situation for himself and other members of the White House staff. He admitted, "The frustration of dealing with a situation in which the schedule of the President of the United States was determined by occult prognostications was very great—far greater than any other I had known in nearly forty-five years of working life."

Soon others outside the immediate White House inner circle also began to have grave reservations about the situation as it was. In 1989 NBC news reporter Andrea Mitchell related the following during a broadcast:

"Intelligence officials say the CIA went nuts when it learned the First Lady was discussing U.S.-Soviet relations with an outsider [Joan Quigley] on nonsecure lines. Some White House officials were also horrified that presidential security was being breached. And, according to former White House officials and Quigley, the astrologer was involved in everything. She picked the departure time for the Reykjavik Summit, the optimum time for signing an arms control treaty, the best time for the trip to Moscow. And, when Mrs. Reagan was upset about a controversial trip to Germany in 1985, Quigley plotted every takeoff and landing. Her scheduling for that visit to the Bitburg cemetery was so complicated that former White House aide Michael Deaver sought permission from Mrs. Reagan to talk to the astrologer directly.... Deaver told NBC News that if Mrs. Reagan wanted a schedule change, she would say, 'I told Ronnie and that's what Joan recommends.'"

Quigley, on the other hand, was no worse for wear and used the publicity concerning her exposure as White House seer to the best of her own advantage, even securing a nice deal for her own memoir. Whether she can actually lay claim to all the accomplishments she listed concerning U.S. policy and international relations is probably a matter better left to future historians rather than paranormal seers and psychics.

Jean Houston

Of the many criticisms leveled at the Clinton administration, too New Age/"woo-woo"/occult would probably not be one of them, at least compared with the previous Republican administrations' affiliations with their stargazing seers. That said, the relationship between

First Lady (and later would-be presidential candidate) Hillary Clinton and Jean Houston deserves some attention.

Jean Houston's authorized biography from her Web site reads:

"Dr. Houston has also served for two years in an advisory capacity to President and Mrs. Clinton as well as helping Mrs. Clinton write *It Takes a Village to Raise a Child*. As a high school student she worked closely with Mrs. [Eleanor] Roosevelt on developing strategies to introduce international awareness and United Nations work to young people. She has also worked with President and Mrs. Carter and counseled leaders in similar positions in numerous countries and cultures. She has worked with several corporations including Xerox, Beatrice Foods, General Electric and Rodale Press. She has also worked with governmental agencies, including the U.S. Department of Commerce, the U.S. Office of Technology Assessment and the Department of Energy."

According to Bob Woodward's 1996 book, *The Choice*, Houston promoted to the First Lady a method of contemplation and self-analysis that seems to be very close to the paranormal process of channeling, whereby one allows an outside spirit to imbue itself in a corporal entity in order to communicate.

According to Woodward's account (which was based on numerous interviews):

ON A VISIT TO the White House in early April 1995, Houston proposed that Hillary search further and dig deeper for her connections to Mrs. Roosevelt. Houston and her work were controversial because she believed in spirits and other worlds, put people into trances and used hypnosis, and because in the 1960s she had conducted experiments with LSD. But she tried to be careful with Hillary and the president, intentionally avoiding any of those techniques.

Houston and [Mary Catherine] Bateson went up with Hillary to the solarium, a sun parlor with three sides of glass windows, perched atop the White House. It was afternoon and they all sat around a circular table, joined by several members of the First Lady's staff. One was making a tape recording of the session. The room, which Hillary had redecorated and which was her favorite place for important meetings, offered a spectacular view to the south of the Washington Monument. Fresh fruit, popcorn and pretzels had been set out.

Houston asked Hillary to imagine she was having a conversation with Eleanor. In her strong and self-confident voice, Houston asked Hillary to shut her eyes in order to eliminate the room and her surroundings, and to bring in as many vivid internal sensory images as possible from her vast knowledge about Eleanor to focus her reflection.

"We admire you," said Houston, who thought Hillary was a great woman. She was trying to create an atmosphere of mutual admiration.

Hillary settled back in her seat, and shut her eyes....

"...You're walking down a hall," Houston said, "and there's Mrs. Roosevelt. Now let's describe her."

Hillary did. She had a wonderful description of Eleanor smiling, outgoing, slightly frumpy, always engaged, always fighting.

"Go there to Mrs. Roosevelt and talk about the possible future of the children," Houston said....

Houston asked the First Lady to open herself up to Mrs. Roosevelt as a way of looking at her own capacities and place in history. Houston regarded it as a classic technique, practiced by Machiavelli, who used to talk to ancient men. "What might Eleanor say? What is your message to her?" she asked Hillary.

Hillary addressed Eleanor focusing on her predecessor's fierceness and determination, her advocacy on behalf of people in need. Hillary continued to address Eleanor, discussing the obstacles, the criticism, the loneliness the former First Lady felt. Her identification with Mrs. Roosevelt was intense and personal....

Houston encouraged Hillary to play the other part, to respond as Mrs. Roosevelt. The discourse with a person not there, particularly an historical figure in an equivalent position, opened up a whole constellation of ideas, Houston felt.

"I was misunderstood," Hillary replied, her eyes still shut, speaking as Mrs. Roosevelt. "You have to do what you think is right," she continued. It was crucial to set a course and hold to it. . . .

Houston said that Hillary needed to see and understand that Mrs. Roosevelt was not just an historic figure but was someone who also was hurt by all that happened to her. And yet Mrs. Roosevelt could go on doing her work. Hillary needed to unleash the same potential in herself. In adversity she needed to inherit from these mythical or historic figures, and to achieve self-healing.

The session, however, was not limited to that single instance of channeling of the former First Lady.

NEXT, HOUSTON ASKED HILLARY to carry on a conversation with Mahatma Gandhi, the Hindu leader, a powerful symbol of stoic self-denial. "Talk to him," Houston said. "What would you say and what would you ask?"

After about an hour, the session was over. . . .

Houston and Bateson said they would be available to meet with Hillary at any time in the future. . . .

But as with administrations dating back to Lincoln and his spiritualists, a degree of confidentiality and deniability were kept in place.

MOST PEOPLE IN THE White House did not know about Hillary's sessions with Houston and Bateson. To some of the few who did, the meetings could trigger politically damaging comparisons to Nancy Reagan's use of astrology, which had heavily influenced if not determined the schedule of her husband, Ronald Reagan. Astrology only changed timing, and it was a kind of pseudoscience that could be fun or worth a laugh. Yet the Reagans had been ridiculed. Hillary's sessions with Houston reflected a serious inner turmoil that she had not resolved. . . .

Hillary continued her meetings and in-depth discussions with Houston and Bateson about the parallels between her life and Eleanor Roosevelt's. . . .

Houston had at least one other deep, reflective meditation session, in which Hillary closed her eyes and carried on imaginary discussion with Eleanor Roosevelt. Houston's purpose was to move forward so Hillary could put her "wounding" in the middle of her story, ending with the birth of a new grace.

Though there is no evidence that these sessions continued beyond that one additional directed session, Houston remained a confidante of the First Lady at least behind the scenes and, as mentioned in her biography, contributed more than a bit to Hillary's No. 1 best-seller, *It Takes a Village.*

Whether she will hold a more public position in some future administration is obviously left to other seers at this point.

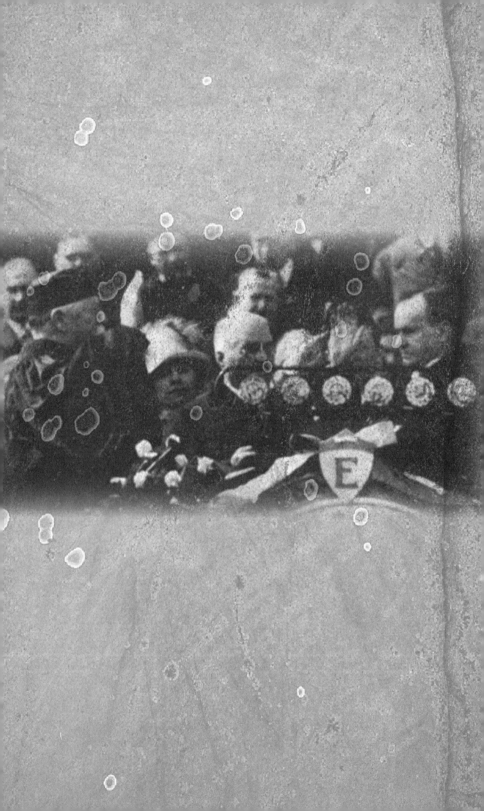

Chapter 14

Silent Cal
Not So Silent after Death

One of the directories of haunted places in America includes a listing for the Renaissance Mayflower Hotel in Washington, D.C. Its listing in *Historic Hotels of America* reads:

"Immediately after its opening in 1925, the Mayflower Hotel was known as the 'Grande Dame of Washington, D.C.,' boasting more gold than any other building in the country except for the Library of Congress. Just four blocks from the White House, this grand, historic hotel remains not only a place to make history but to absorb it; throughout the last 80 years the hotel has hosted events that have changed the course of human affairs. An 'inaugural address' in the truest sense of the term, the hotel has hosted every U.S. Presidential inaugural ball since Calvin Coolidge."

That first inaugural ball, however, was one the president didn't actually attend, though it has been reported that he has made up for this absence many times over by attending on numerous occasions after his death.

Coolidge's White House biography is fairly succinct: "As President, Coolidge demonstrated his determination to preserve the old moral and economic precepts amid the material prosperity which many Americans were enjoying. He refused to use Federal economic power to check the growing boom or to ameliorate the depressed condition of agriculture and certain industries. His first message to Congress in December 1923 called for isolation in foreign policy, and for tax cuts, economy, and limited aid to farmers. He rapidly became popular. In 1924, as the beneficiary of what was becoming known as 'Coolidge prosperity,' he polled more than 54 percent of the popular vote. In his Inaugural he asserted that the country had achieved 'a state of contentment seldom before seen,' and pledged himself to maintain the status quo. In subsequent years he twice vetoed farm relief bills, and killed a plan to produce cheap Federal electric power on the Tennessee River. The political genius of President Coolidge, Walter Lippmann pointed out in 1926, was his talent for effectively doing nothing: 'This active inactivity suits the mood and certain of the needs of the country admirably. It suits all the business interests which want to be let alone. . . . And it suits all those who have become convinced that government in this country has become dangerously complicated and top-heavy. . . .' "

Always ready to be photographed but seldom willing to say anything, let alone anything of note or on the record, "Silent Cal" (as he was called) was a hands-off president, but the outward contentment he showed the nation masked an inner turmoil that haunted his own personal life.

At the end of June 1924, Coolidge's two sons, John and Cal Jr., played a rousing game of tennis. Unfortunately, Cal Jr. (the younger brother) neglected to wear socks with his tennis shoes, resulting in the formation of a rather large blister on one of his toes. The toe quickly became quite infected, sepsis set in, and the young man died of blood poisoning within a week as his horrified family watched helplessly. Cal Jr. was only sixteen at the time and up to that point had been considered to be in better than good health.

The president immediately became depressed and refrained from occasions that were of a less than serious or necessary nature (as he was a firm conservative, this was also perfectly in keeping with his "less government is more" point of view).

One of the areas that he made sure fell into this "less is more" category was his own inaugural celebration. Not surprisingly, winning the election failed to bolster the spirits of the still-grieving parent.

From *Time* magazine December 8, 1924: "The prospect of a 'modest inaugural' began to take form. The inaugural ball Mr. Coolidge had already vetoed. Last week a curtailed parade was agreed upon. It is probable that if the President had consulted his own wishes alone, there would have been no parade. But Washington merchants, who find great profit in the inauguration ceremonies, pressed very earnestly for more display." And though the balls did eventually go on at such places as the Mayflower Hotel, the president did not attend . . . at least then. It has been reliably reported that every year on January 20, the date of the inaugural ball, strange things happen at the hotel: The lights dim and flicker at 10:00 p.m., the time when guests of honor at the ball are announced; one elevator stops at the eighth floor until 10:15 p.m., when Coolidge would have left his room to come down to the ball; the elevator then descends to the lobby level.

After being reunited with his son, Coolidge no longer had a reason to mourn or miss out on any of the festivities at hand.

The Presidents and the UFOs

In his memoir, *Friends in High Places: Our Journey from Little Rock to Washington, D.C.*, the former U.S. associate attorney general in the Clinton administration, Webb Hubbell, claims that there were certain specific truths he was asked to uncover by the forty-second president. On page 282 of the book he recalls "something the President had asked me to do when I was first elected. 'Webb,' he had said, 'if I put you over at justice, I want you to find the answers to two questions for me. One, Who killed JFK? And two, Are there UFOs?' He was dead serious."

Indeed, the subject of UFOs and the presidency has been of great interest since that fateful day in Roswell, New Mexico. On July 8, 1947, it was reported that personnel from the U.S. Air Force 509th Bomb Group had recovered a crashed "flying disc," which over the years has led to speculation that a spacecraft from another world was recovered, complete with the bodies of its alien crew.

Harry S Truman

A 1995 GAO report (U.S. General Accounting Office/Washington, DC 20545/National Security and International Affairs Division/B-262046), almost fifty years after the fact, summed up the facts of the event:

ON JULY 8, 1947, the Roswell Army Air Field (RAAF) public information office in Roswell, New Mexico, reported the crash and recovery of a "flying disc." Army Air Forces personnel from the RAAF's 509th Bomb Group were credited with the recovery. The following day, the press reported that the Commanding General of the U.S. Eighth Air Force, Fort Worth, Texas, announced that RAAF personnel had recovered a crashed radar-tracking (weather) balloon, not a flying disc.

After nearly 50 years, speculation continues on what crashed at Roswell. Some observers believe that the object was of extraterrestrial origin. In the July 1994 "Report of Air Force Research Regarding the Roswell Incident," the Air Force did not dispute that something happened near Roswell, but reported that the most likely source of the wreckage was from a balloon-launched classified government project designed to determine the state of Soviet nuclear weapons research. The debate on what crashed at Roswell continues....

In our search for records concerning the Roswell crash, we learned that some government records covering RAAF activities had been destroyed and others had not. For example, RAAF administrative records (from Mar. 1945 through Dec. 1949) and RAAF outgoing messages (from Oct. 1946 through Dec. 1949) were destroyed. The document disposition form does not indicate what organization or person destroyed the records and when or under what authority the records were destroyed.

"Our search for government records concerning the Roswell crash yielded two records originating in 1947—a July 1947 history report by the combined 509th Bomb Group and RAAF and an FBI teletype message dated July 8, 1947. The 509th-RAAF report noted the recovery of a "flying disc" that was later determined by military officials to be a radar-tracking balloon. The FBI message stated that the military had reported that an object resembling a high-altitude weather balloon with a radar reflector had been recovered near Roswell.

The other government records we reviewed, including those previously withheld from the public because of security classification, and the Air Force's analysis of unidentified flying object sightings from 1946 to 1953 (Project Blue Book Special Report No. 14), did not mention the crash or the recovery of an airborne object near Roswell in July 1947. Similarly, executive branch agencies' responses to our letters of inquiry produced no other government records on the Roswell crash.

Even fifty years afterward, there is not a documented assessment of all the facts concerning this event and the involvement of the military and the executive branch of the government in its investigation. This fuels the speculation about secret UFO files involving the president.

Truman has been quoted as saying, "I can assure you that flying saucers, given that they exist, are not constructed by any power on earth" . . . further fueling the debate on these matters. According to a 1996 Associated Press story titled "UFO Believers Seek Clues at Presidential Libraries":

TELEPHONE CALLS AND VISITS by "UFOlogists" have been a workplace reality at the Dwight D. Eisenhower and Harry S. Truman presidential libraries since the mid-1980s. That's when stories of a downed UFO in July 1947 near Roswell Army Air Field started circulating in earnest.

The researchers who frequent the Eisenhower library in Abilene, Kan., and the Truman library in Independence, Mo., often are looking for information about the whereabouts of the two presidents on certain dates, among other things, library staff members said.

UFO researchers also inquire about the authenticity of a Nov. 18, 1952, briefing paper allegedly prepared for Eisenhower, elected president days before.

The document appears to detail a federal panel known as Majestic-12, or MJ-12, allegedly established by Truman to investigate the crash in Roswell.

The archivists at both libraries have little to show the research- ers. Nor are they inclined to verify the authenticity of the various genuine-looking documents presented them by UFOlogists.

The lack of facts and documentation has, of course, led to the wild- est matters of speculation (which has undoubtedly led to the popular- ity of conspiracy theories and fictive accounts such as *The X-Files* TV series). Perhaps one of the most popular of these theories involved the thirty-fourth president, Dwight David Eisenhower, who supposedly viewed the alien bodies that were recovered at Roswell or had a diplo- matic meeting with an emissary from their home planet.

Dwight David Eisenhower

A March 29, 1989, article by William Moore in the *Hollywood Gazette* summarized the most suspicious related event during his presidency:

THE STORY TAKES MANY forms, with the common thread being that Ike mysteriously disappeared one evening while on a vacation to Palm Springs, and that he was spirited to Edwards to view (or meet) aliens. It is said that he returned by dawn and shortly thereafter ordered absolute secrecy about anything having to do with UFOs. No doubt one of the reasons that this particular rumor has continued to circulate for such a long time is that there are a number of verifiable facts associated with it—some of them rather curious.

For example, President Eisenhower did indeed make a trip to Palm Springs between February 17th and 24th, 1954, and on the evening of Saturday, February 20th, he did disappear! When members of the press learned that the president was not where he should be, rumors ran rampant that he had either died or was seriously ill.

The story even managed to get onto a press wire before being killed moments later. To quell the fuss, White House Press Secretary James Haggerty called an urgent late evening press conference to announce "solemnly" that the president had been enjoying fried chicken earlier that evening, had knocked a cap off a tooth, and had been taken to a local dentist for treatment.

When Ike turned up as scheduled the next morning for an early church service, the matter seemed ended. Although the Palm Springs trip was billed as a "vacation for the president," the trip appears to have come up rather suddenly. In addition, it is a matter of record that Ike had returned from a quail shooting vacation in Georgia less than a week before leaving for Palm Springs.

Another Eisenhower UFO incident that was reported by no less than the *New York Post* in 1997 suggests that the soon-to-be president actually encountered a UFO during his military service. The incident took place in 1952 and was related by a crew member serving on Ike's flagship:

WE WERE NORTH AND EAST of England with the NATO fleet in the North Atlantic. About 1:30 a.m., through the stormy rain and lightning, this big blue-white light appeared right off starboard bow. It came down to 100 feet of the water and just hung there as we cruised by it.

This UFO was easy to see when the lightning flashed. It then rose straight and left. Four of us saw it. Here's the kicker! General Ike, who'd flown over by chopper with the Admiral, had just come out on the signal bridge wearing PJ's and robe, looking for coffee.

We were sitting and making small talk when the bright light came on. We all watched it ten minutes, then just stood there staring at each other. After a while, Gen. Eisenhower said, he better go 'check this out' and left. He also told us to 'forget about it for now.'

Next day and ever after, nothing was ever said about it. I don't know what it was or why it was hushed, but I saw it.

Johnson, Nixon, and Ford

Ironically, the advent of NASA (National Aeronautics and Space Administration) in 1958 seems to have caused a lull in UFO-presidential linkages. The American public became enthralled in the so-called space race and the Kennedy challenge to land a man on the moon by the end of the decade, perhaps signaling that they were willing to wait to discover the facts of the matter once we got there, namely the moon and beyond.

According to several letters in his archives, Lyndon Johnson continually expressed a willingness to "investigate all responsible reports and claims of evidence" concerning UFOs, though little if any follow-up on his part seems to have come to pass.

There is also an apocryphal story in the *National Enquirer* on August 16, 1983, that Johnson's successor, Richard Nixon, once showed the Roswell alien bodies to his good friend, entertainer Jackie Gleason.

On a trip to Florida in February 1973, Nixon attended a charity golf tournament run by Gleason. Nixon ditched his Secret Service escort (a common practice for him when he was in friendly territory and wanted his privacy) so he could drive a car right up to the Gleason estate. It is alleged that he picked the "Great One" up and drove him to a nearby Air Force base to show his high-profile friend the evidence of the extraterrestrials. Though the story is sourced to Gleason's wife, it is far from credible given its lack of additional confirming sources.

Nixon's successor was probably not around long enough to investigate the matter, though a quote from his earlier congressional career indicates that had he had time he might have been so inclined. On March 25, 1966, then House Minority Leader Gerald Ford said, "I believe Congress should thoroughly investigate the rash of reported sightings of unidentified flying objects in Southern Michigan and other parts of the country. I feel a congressional inquiry would be most worthwhile because the American people are intensely interested in the UFO stories, and some people are alarmed by them. Air Force investigators have been checking on such reports for years but have come up with nothing very conclusive. In the light of these new sightings and incidents near Ann Arbor, Michigan, and elsewhere, it would be a very wholesome thing for a committee of the Congress to conduct hearings and to call responsible witnesses from the executive branch of the government and other witnesses who say they have sighted these objects. I think the American people would feel better if there was a full-blown investigation of these mysterious flying objects, which some persons honestly believe that they have seen."

The next elected president, however, provided his own public documentation for his UFO encounter and is indeed on record as the first official corroborated presidential UFO connection.

Jimmy Carter

According to Howell Raines in the *Atlanta Constitution* (September 14, 1973), then-Governor Jimmy Carter confirmed to the public that he had actually seen an unidentified flying object and filed an official report on the matter.

It occurred in the town of Leary, Georgia, while then-candidate Carter was campaigning at a local Lions Club. He called it a very sober event and immediately took notes on the occasion with a tape recorder, including specific details of what he saw and described as a "very remarkable sight." ("It was about 30 degrees above the horizon and looked about as large as the moon. It got smaller and changed to a reddish color and then got larger again," Carter recalled.)

An abridged transcription of the actual UFO report as filed by Carter is as follows (note: several of the entries were left blank, and multiple-choice entries are designated by underlining):

```
Name:  Jimmy Carter
Address:  State Capitol, Atlanta
Occupation:  Governor
Education:  Graduate
Special Training:  Nuclear Physics
Military Service:  U.S. Navy
Date of observation:  October, 1969
Time:  7:15 P.M. E.S.T. Location:  Leary, Georgia
How long did you see the object? 10–12 minutes.
Weather conditions and type of sky:
    shortly after dark.
Position of sun or moon with respect to the
    object and to you:  not in sight.
Were the stars or moon visible? stars.
More than one object? no.


PLEASE DESCRIBE THE OBJECT(S) IN DETAIL. . . .
Please use additional sheets of paper if
necessary.
    Was the object brighter than the
        background of the sky? yes.
    Compare the brightness with the sun, moon,
        headlights, etc.:  At one time as bright as moon.
    Did the object:
        Appear to stand still at any time? yes.
```

Suddenly speed up and rush away at any
time?

Break up into two parts or explode?

Give off smoke?

Leave any visible trail?

Drop anything?

Change brightness? **yes.**

Change shape? **size.**

Change color? **yes.**

Seemed to move toward us from a distance

Stop move partially away, return. Then

depart. Bluish at first. Then reddish.

Luminous—not solid.

Did the object(s) at any time pass in front
of, or behind of, anything? **no.**

Was there any wind? **no.**

Did you observe the object(s) through
an optical instrument or other aid,
windshield, windowpane,. . . . **no.**

Did the object(s) have any sound? **no.**

Please tell if the objects were:

A. Fuzzy or blurred

B. Like a bright star

C. Sharply outlined

Was the object:

A. Self luminous

B. Dull finish

C. Reflecting

D. Transparent

NOTICE Please draw, to the best of your
ability, a sketch of the object(s), including
all details. You may use extra sheet.

Did the object(s) rise or fall while in
motion? Came close, moved away. Came close, then moved
away.

Tell the apparent size of the objects when
compared with the following held at arm's
length: Pinhead, pea, ... About same as moon
maybe a little smaller. Varied from brighter/larger than planet
to apparent size of moon.

How did you happen to notice the objects?
10–12 men all watched it. Brightness attracted us.

Where were you and what were you doing at the
time? Outside waiting for a meeting to begin at 7:30 PM.

How did the object(s) disappear from view?
Moved to distance. Then disappeared.

Compare the speed of the object(s) with
a piston or jet aircraft at the same
apparent altitude: not pertinent.

Were there any conventional aircraft in
the location at the time or immediately
afterward? no.

Please estimate the distance of the
object(s). Difficult—maybe 300 to 1000 yards.

What was the elevation of the object(s) in
the sky? About 30 degrees above horizon.

Names and addresses of other witnesses, if
any: 10 members of Leary, Ga., Lions Club.

Please draw a map of the locality of the
observation, showing North. . . . Please
use extra sheet for map and attach to
form. Appeared from west about 30 degrees up.

Is there an airport, military, governmental,
or research installation in the area? no.

Have you seen other objects of an unidentified
nature? no.
Please enclose photographs, motion pictures,
newspaper clippings. . . .
Were you interrogated by Air Force
Investigators? By any other Federal,
state, ... no.
Were you asked or told not to reveal or
discuss the incident? If so, . . . no.
We would like your permission to quote your
name in connection with this report . . .
However, if you prefer, we will keep your
name confidential . . . Please note your
choice by checking the proper statement
below . . .

        You may use my name
        Please keep my name confidential
Date of filling out this report: 9/18/73
Signature: [signed] Jimmy Carter

A subsequent article in the *Humanist* magazine in 1977 attempted to refute then-President Carter's recollection of the event and dismiss his UFO sighting. Robert Sheaffer, a member of the UFO Subcommittee of the Committee for the Scientific Investigation of Claims of the Paranormal, concluded that "Mr. Carter reports that his 'UFO' was in the western sky, at about 30 degrees elevation. This almost perfectly matches the known position of Venus, which was in the west-southwest at an altitude of 25 degrees. Weather records show that the sky was clear at the time of the sighting. . . . No other object generates as many UFO reports as the planet Venus. Venus is not as bright as the moon, nor does it actually approach the viewer, or change size and brightness, but descriptions like these are typical of misidentifications of a bright planet. Every time Venus reaches its maximum brilliance in the evening sky, hundreds of 'UFO sightings' of this type are made. At the time of the Carter UFO sighting, Venus was a brilliant evening star, nearly one hundred times brighter than a first-magnitude star."

Though well reasoned, however, Sheaffer's conclusions are only as valid as Carter's concerning this matter, and numerous attempts to use the UFO report as a means for derision or mode for undermining the former president's credibility and cognitive abilities all overlook a simple detail. Carter never claimed to see anything extraterrestrial, alien, or paranormal in nature. What he saw was indeed an unidentified flying object and he reported it as such, leaving the matter of its further identification for those more qualified. Filing the UFO report was in fact the reasoned judgment of a rational man, and exactly what an observer—whether he be a skeptic or a "true believer"—is expected to do.

And in a coincidence worthy of Jinxy McDeath himself, Carter's GOP successor to the White House also had a UFO experience while serving as governor.

Ronald Reagan

According to an article by A. Hovni in *UFO Universe* (September 1988): "There is an unconfirmed story that before he became Governor of California, Ron and Nancy Reagan had a UFO sighting on a highway near Hollywood. The story was broadcast last February on Steve Allen's radio show over WNEW-AM in New York. The comedian and host commented that a very well known personality in the entertainment industry had confided to him that many years ago, Ron and Nancy were expected to a casual dinner with friends in Hollywood. Except for the Reagans, all the guests had arrived. Ron and Nancy showed up quite upset half an hour later, saying that they had just seen a UFO coming down the coast. No further details were released by Steve Allen."

Additional details were available through UFOhelpfiles.com: "It was 1974, and he was governor of California. He was being flown in a small plane, a Cessna, to a party and just over Bakersfield he and his pilot, Bill Poynter, spotted a UFO. The UFO started out as a glowing white light several hundred yards from the plane, changed shape and became elongated, then began departing. It moved slowly at first; then in a second or so it gained incredible speed and disappeared."

Unlike Carter, however, Reagan seems to have kept the UFO incident on the front burner and indeed allowed it to influence his presidential policy-making. In his first summit with then–General Secretary of the Communist Party of the Soviet Union Mikhail Sergeyevich Gorbachev, the fortieth president of the United States noted, according to the official White House transcript, "How easy his task and mine might be in these meetings that we held if suddenly there was a threat to this world from some other species from another planet outside in the universe. We'd forget all the little local differences that we have between our countries. . . ."

Reagan drove this point home in a speech before the U.N. General Assembly on September 21, 1987, saying, "In our obsession with antagonisms of the moment, we often forget how much unites all the members of humanity. Perhaps we need some outside, universal threat to make us recognize this common bond. . . . I occasionally think, how quickly our differences worldwide would vanish if we were facing an alien threat from outside this world. And yet, I ask is not an alien force already among us? What could be more alien to the universal aspirations of our peoples than war and the threat of war?"

Given the fact that one of his administration's key initiatives was a defense system known as Star Wars that was supposedly inspired by Reagan's own conversation with a noted California science fiction author (who may or may not have been actually taking the matter seriously in terms of public policy rather than typical fictioneer blue fabulation) concerning the mounting of missiles, lasers, and other weaponry on orbiting space platforms to "defend the United States from the high ground from its enemies on Earth and elsewhere," one has no alternative but to assume that, unlike cautious skeptic Carter, Ronald Reagan was indeed a UFO true believer.

William Jefferson Clinton

And of course as evidenced by Webb Hubbell's memoir, the forty-second president, William Jefferson Clinton, was also interested in at least the general subject of UFOs. There is even movie footage of him commenting on the apparent SETI contact with Earth. His exact words are: "This is the product of years of exploration by some of the world's most distinguished scientists. . . . If this discovery is confirmed, it will surely be one of the most stunning insights into our universe that science has uncovered. Its implications are as far reaching and awe-inspiring as can be imagined. . . ."

There is no doubt the president said these words; however, their connection to alien contact is entirely fictional. In actuality the words were said in reference to a press release related to a scientific discovery of an evidentiary artifact connected to a Mars meteor that may or may not provide a "biological fingerprint" of life on other planets. It's a significant discovery, but far from conclusive or even necessarily revelatory.

His words became linked to the SETI project through the marvels of special effects and moviemaking by Robert Zemeckis. The director responsible for such similar gimmick films as *Who Framed Roger Rabbit* and *Forrest Gump,* Zemeckis edited the president's appearance into the movie *Contact* to evoke a verisimilitude for the fictional film based on Carl Sagan's novel, much to the chagrin of the White House and its Office of Legal Counsel.

This notwithstanding, a recent (November 2007) article in *Time* magazine dealing with Freedom of Information Act (FOIA) requests from the Clinton archives have indicated that neither his "impeachment happy" and "Hillary bashing" detractors nor his idolizing supporters were the first to deluge archives with requests for information.

Indeed, it was the self-proclaimed UFOlogists who first requested copies of all materials related to UFOs; Roswell, New Mexico; flying saucers; Area 51; or the TV show *X-Files.*

To date, these requests have yielded:

FOIA REQUEST 2006-0490-F consists of correspondence from "The Project Starlight Coalition" to President Clinton and a response from James A. Dorskind, Special Assistant to the President/Director of Correspondence and Presidential Messages, regarding unidentified flying objects and extraterrestrials. WHORM Subject File FE010-01 contains a letter, dated June 4, 1995, to President Clinton from "The Project Starlight Coalition." Edgar Mitchell is one of many signatories on this letter. The file also contains a letter, dated August 3, 1995, from James A. Dorskind, to Steven M. Greer, M.D., Director, Center for the Study of Extraterrestrial Intelligence regarding unidentified flying objects and extraterrestrials.

FOIA REQUEST 2006-0492-F consists of emails to and from John Podesta, containing the words either, X-Files or Area 51. John Podesta was a renowned fan of the *X-Files* television show. Automated Records Management System (ARMS) contains emails with many passing remarks about the *X-Files* during 1998 and 1999. Additionally, there are several emails that contain articles regarding the *X-Files* television show.

FOIA REQUEST 2006-0530-F consists of correspondence from "The Project Starlight Coalition" to President Clinton and a response from James A. Dorskind, Special Assistant to the President/

Director of Correspondence and Presidential Messages, regarding unidentified flying objects and extraterrestrials. WHORM Subject File FE010-01 contains a letter, dated June 4, 1995, to President Clinton from "The Project Starlight Coalition." Marie (Bootsie) Galbraith is one of many signatories on this letter. The file also contains a letter, dated August 3, 1995, from James A. Dorskind, to Steven M. Greer, M.D., Director, Center for the Study of Extraterrestrial Intelligence regarding unidentified flying objects and extraterrestrials.

FOIA REQUEST 2006-0531-F consists of correspondence from "The Project Starlight Coalition" to President Clinton and a response from James A. Dorskind, Special Assistant to the president/Director of Correspondence and Presidential Messages, regarding unidentified flying objects and extraterrestrials. WHORM Subject File FE010-01 contains a letter, dated June 4, 1995, to President Clinton from "The Project Starlight Coalition." Steven Greer is one of many signatories on this letter. The file also contains a letter, dated August 3, 1995, from James A. Dorskind, to Steven M. Greer, M.D., Director, Center for the Study of Extraterrestrial Intelligence regarding unidentified flying objects and extraterrestrials.

FOIA REQUEST 2006-0535-F consists of email forwards that contain Mike McCurry in the list of recipients, containing the word UFO. Automated Records Management System (ARMS) contains a memo emailed from Mark Neschis to Mike McCurry, Ann Lewis and Rahm Emanuel dated July 2, 1998 regarding the weekend television schedule for July 3-5, 1998. Additionally, an email forwarded by Margaret M. Suntum to twenty-one people, including Mike McCurry, dated April 6, 1998 contains an internal transcript of President Clinton's remarks at the National Newspaper Association Reception in the East Room of the White House March 20, 1998.

[And my personal favorite:]

FOIA REQUEST 2006-0543-F regarding records
or correspondence related to President Clinton wanting the Sci-
Fi Channel at the White House and Camp David (consists of an
email regarding the Sci-Fi Channel at Camp David. Automated Records Management System (ARMS) contains an email from Patricia
F. Lewis to Mary Ellen Glynn and Virginia M. Terzano dated June 14,
1996 regarding the Sci-Fi Channel at Camp David).

Needless to say, nothing of an earth- and/or other planet–shaking
nature has been uncovered so far.

It is also worth noting that the subject of UFOs actually entered into
the 2007 Democratic presidential candidate debates.

Word has leaked out that in actress and New Age advocate Shir-
ley MacLaine's latest book, *Sage-ing While Age-ing*, liberal-minded
Democratic congressman and presidential hopeful Dennis Kucinich
observed a UFO while visiting the Washington state–based actress,
who is his daughter's godmother. As a result, during the Philadelphia-
based debate the NBC moderator, Tim Russert, the former host of
Meet the Press, questioned him on this topic.

Kucinich did not dodge the question.

He replied: "It was an unidentified flying object, OK? It's, like,
it's unidentified. I saw something. [*pause to acknowledge laughter*] I'm
also going to move my campaign office to Roswell, New Mexico, and
another one in Exeter, New Hampshire, OK? And also, you have to
keep in mind that more—that Jimmy Carter saw a UFO and also that
more people in this country have seen UFOs than I think approve of
George Bush's presidency."

The Roswell reference was fairly obvious, and the Exeter reference relates to a well-documented UFO sighting that occurred in September 1965.

Afterword

When I was a lad I remember staying up late one night to watch the old program *One Step Beyond*. The show was a Believe It or Not sort of drama series featuring *Twilight Zone*–type tales of the uncanny that were purported to actually be true.

The program that night (which of course gave me nightmares) dealt with some of the supernatural details of the Lincoln assassination, specifically his death dream. Scares aside, I was intrigued . . . and soon found myself immersed in the comic strips based on *Ripley's Believe It or Not* and whatever else the Scholastic Book Club had to offer on the subject of the paranormal and its slightly more mystic moniker, the occult.

Author/researchers such as Hans Holzer, Peter Haining, Victor Canning, Charles Berlitz, etc., added to the breadth of my knowledge on this subject.

Some of the accounts were lurid.

Some of the accounts were spooky.

. . . and some of the accounts definitely fell into the category of being pretty unbelievable.

Rational minds had to dismiss such matters . . . yet many brilliant minds were not so fast to dismiss such things that encroached on the unknown, and for every scoffer in one area there is a tangential supporter in another.

Nowhere did this collision of ideas mash-up better than in high school, where the esteemed Jesuits taught me the rational approach of the scientific method, side by side with confirmation that the so-called rites of exorcism did exist and were still practiced to this day (this was the era of William Peter Blatty's *Exorcist,* after all).

What this taught me was simple—have a critical eye, a discriminating ear, and an open mind.

No matter how well documented a given event, there is always room for the unknown.

Do UFOs exist?

Of course, since *UFO* only means "unidentified flying object."

Is it anti-Christian to believe in the existence of devils and prophecy?

How can it be when there is evidence of both in the New Testament?

Sir Arthur C. Clarke possibly summed matters up best in two quotes:

- "Any sufficiently advanced technology is indistinguishable from magic."
- "The truth, as always, will be far stranger."

I for one have always preferred the definition of occult as "hidden."

And as long as there is something hidden, history will always be worth looking into.

Acknowledgments

Special thanks to William B. Fawcett, William Terdoslavich, James Fallone, my Jesuit educators, my editor Lane Butler, my agent Frank Weimann (and his paranormally helpful staff), my loving wife, Donna, and, of course, Minx the three-legged wonder cat.

Any errors are mine alone (but probably ascribable to forces beyond the realm of mortal men).

Sourced Materials

(In most cases the citations are included in the text, though additional material citations are herewith provided for the following chapters.)

INTRODUCTION
"Exorcism: Beating the Devil" by Sally Quinn, *Washington Post*, November 6, 1972.

CHAPTER 1 The Visions of Washington
"Recollections and Private Memoirs of Washington" by George Washington Parke Custis, Mary Randolph Custis Lee; "George Washington's Remarkable Vision," originally published by Wesley Bradshaw in *National Review* 4 (December 1880); "General McClellan's Vision of George Washington," *National Tribune* (December 1880).

CHAPTER 4 The First Ladies' Haunted Homes
"Playing Host to Ghosts" by Phil Casey, *Washington Post*, May 4, 1969; "Gov. Carter's Wife: Jimmy and I Lived in a Haunted House for Five Years" by Shelley Ross, *National Enquirer*, April 27, 1976; "Rosalynn Carter's Haunted House," *Examiner*, May 3, 1983.

CHAPTER 13 The Twentieth-Century Presidents and Their Seers
"In Strasburg, A Medium Well Done" by Sean Daly, *Washington Post*, July 31, 2002.

CHAPTER 15 The Presidents and the UFOs
www.ufoevidence.org/documents/doc845.htm; "President Carter's 'UFO' Is Identified as the Planet Venus" by Robert Sheaffer, *Humanist*, July–August, 1977; "Learyites Leery of Carter's Encounter" by Tom Tiede, *Mt. Pleasant (Texas) Daily Tribune*, February 2, 1978; "Carter Once Saw a UFO on 'Very Sober Occasion'" by Howell Raines, *Atlanta Constitution*, September 14, 1973; "The Shocking Truth: Ronald Reagan's Obsession with an Alien Invasion" by A. Hovni, *UFO Universe*, September 1988.

Select Bibliography

Alexander, John. *Ghosts—Washington Revisited: The Ghostlore of the Nation's Capital.* Atglen, Pa.: Schiffer, 1998.

Beyer, Rick. *The Greatest Presidential Stories Never Told: 100 Tales from History to Astonish, Bewilder, and Stupefy.* New York: HarperCollins, 2007.

Blum, Deborah. *Ghost Hunters: William James and the Search for Scientific Proof of Life After Death.* New York: Penguin, 2006.

Bugliosi, Vincent. *Reclaiming History: The Assassination of President John F. Kennedy.* New York: Norton, 2007.

Cayce, Edgar. *My Life as a Seer—The Lost Memoirs.* New York: Saint Martin's, 2002.

Craughwell, Thomas J. *Stealing Lincoln's Body.* Cambridge, Mass.: Harvard University Press, 2007.

Dixon, Jeane, and Rene Noorbergen. *Jeane Dixon: My Life and Prophecies.* New York: William Morrow, 1969.

Ebon, Martin, ed. *Exorcism: Fact Not Fiction.* New York: New American Library, 1974.

Fawcett, Bill. *Oval Office Oddities.* New York: HarperCollins, 2008.

Hieronimus, Robert, and Laura Cortner. *Founding Fathers, Secret Societies: Freemasons, Illuminati, Rosicrucians, and the Decoding of the Great Seal.* Rochester, Vt.: Destiny Books, 2006.

Hoagland, Richard, and Mike Bara. *Dark Mission: The Secret History of NASA.* Los Angeles: Feral House, 2007.

Holmes, David L. *The Faiths of the Founding Fathers.* New York: Oxford University Press, 2006.

Holzer, Hans. *White House Ghosts.* New York: Leisure Books, 1979.

Hubbell, Webster. *Friends in High Places: Our Journey from Little Rock to Washington, D.C.* New York: William Morrow & Co., 1997.

Kachuba, John. *Ghosthunters: On the Trail of Mediums, Dowsers, Spirit Seekers, and Other Investigations of America's Paranormal World.* Franklin Lakes, N.J.: Career Press, 2007.

Kirkpatrick, Sidney. *Edgar Cayce: An American Prophet.* New York: Riverhead Books, 2000.

Kurtz, Katherine. *Two Crowns for America.* New York: Bantam, 1996.

Martin, Joel, and William J. Birnes. *The Haunting of the Presidents: A Paranormal History of the U.S. Presidency.* New York: New American Library, 2003.

Meltzer, Brad. *The Book of Fate.* New York: Warner Books, 2007.

O'Brien, Cormac. *Secret Lives of the First Ladies.* Philadelphia: Quirk Books, 2005.

O'Brien, Cormac/ *Secret Lives of the U.S. Presidents.* Philadelphia: Quirk Books, 2004.

Quigley, Joan. *What Does Joan Say? My Seven Years as White House Astrologer to Nancy and Ronald Reagan.* New York: Birch Lane Press, 1992.

Regan, Donald. *For the Record.* New York: Harcourt, 1988.

Schneck, Robert Damon. *The President's Vampire (Strange-but-True Tales of the United States of America).* New York: Barnes & Noble, 2007.

Smith, Warren. *Into the Strange.* New York: Popular Library, 1968.

Taylor, Troy. *The Haunted President: The History, Hauntings & Supernatural Life of Abraham Lincoln (Haunted Illinois).* Decatur, Ill.: Whitechapel Productions, 2005.

Vowell, Sara. *Assassination Vacation.* New York: Simon & Schuster, 2005.

Woodward, Bob. *The Choice.* New York: Simon & Schuster, 1996.

U.S. News & World Report: Mysteries of History—Secret Societies. New York: U.S. News & World Report, 2007.

AS WELL AS THE FOLLOWING PUBLIC DOMAIN WORKS:

"The Diary and Remembrances" of the Reverend Nathaniel Randolph Snowden.

Recollections and Private Memoirs of Washington by George Washington Parke Custis and Mary Randolph Custis Lee. Washington D.C.: William H. Moore (publisher), 1859.

"General McClellan's Vision of George Washington," *Evening Courier,* Portland, Maine, March 8, 1862.

"Interior Causes of the War: The Nation Demonized, and Its President a Spirit-Rapper," by 1863 Citizen of Ohio, Cornell University Library, January 1, 1863.

"A Readable Sketch: Spiritualism at the White House" by Prior Melton, *Herald of Progress,* May 1863.

"Lincoln's Dream," *Harper's New Monthly Magazine,* 1864.

"Vision of Washington" at Valley Forge as supposedly told by a gentleman named Anthony Sherman, *National Tribune* 4 (December 1880).

History of an Attempt to Steal the Body of Abraham Lincoln by John Carroll Power, ed., Springfield, Ill.: H. W. Rokker, 1890.

Lincoln: An Account of His Personal Life, Especially of Its Springs of Action as Revealed and Deepened by the Ordeal of War by Nathaniel Wright Stephenson. Indianapolis, Ind.: The Bobbs-Merrill Company Publishers, 1922.

"Through Blood and Fire at Gettysburg" by Joshua Chamberlain, *Hearst's Magazine*, June 1913.

Was Abraham Lincoln a Spiritualist?: Or, Curious Revelations from the Life of a Trance Medium by Nettie Colburn Maynard. Philadelphia: R. C. Hartranft (publisher), 1891.

And information provided by the federal government pertaining to official records, and matters of public interest at the White House, the Octagon House, Valley Forge, and the Smithsonian Institution.